Outdoor Grub

carol tennant

Outdoor Grub

carol tennant

hot n' spicy **barbecue**

MQP

birds
of a feather

14

Published by MQ Publications Limited
12 The Ivories, 6–8 Northampton Street
London N1 2HY
Tel: +44 (0) 20 7359 2244
Fax:+44 (0) 20 7359 1616
email: mail@mqpublications.com
website: www.mqpublications.com

Text: Copyright © 2003 Carol Tennant
Editor: Yvonne Deutch
Design: Lindsey Johns, Design Revolution

ISBN: 1-84072-459-5

10 9 8 7 6 5 4 3 2 1

Printed and bound in China

gone
fishin'

84

contents

Through the retro years of the late 40s and 50s the rugged outdoors tradition of simple campfire food gradually evolved into mainstream barbecue cooking, as patio grills became easily available. Since then, our enthusiasm for barbecue fare has become ever more intense—and the 50s craze for outdoor eating has never been more popular than it is today!

Meanwhile, our passion for hot and spicy flavors has flourished unabated; that's why **OUTDOOR GRUB: hot n' spicy barbecue** is so timely. You can recreate the era of friendly retro backyard barbecues, and also savor a dazzling array of outdoor dishes that get your taste buds dancing with the sheer excitement of sizzling hot new flavors. So, now that you've got yourself all fired up and ready to get out there and cook up a storm, check out these useful guidelines on how to get the best from your barbecue.

Gas or charcoal?

There are arguments for and against both of these fuels, and proponents of each will be quick to list them.

CHARCOAL gives more flavor because the meat juices drip directly onto the coals, providing its own smoke and the flavor that comes with it. A kettle barbecue is a good choice, as this type is affordable, easy to light, simple to control, and can be used both for direct and indirect grilling. Charcoal is also a lot easier to use if you're out and about on vacation, and may need to set up a barbecue while you're on the move. It's also useful to know that many of the recipes in this book can be cooked over an open fire, if necessary.

GAS GRILLS are popular because they provide instant, controllable heat. They, too, are easy to light and can be used for direct and indirect grilling. They tend to be a little more expensive, though economy versions are increasingly available. And they're a lot easier to use for long cooking times because you don't have to tend the fire as closely—you should still make sure you have a spare canister on hand, though, in case you run out mid-way.

Other useful equipment

Useful items for the barbecue cook include an oven mitt for moving the grill around, or for adding coals during indirect charcoal cooking. Long-handled utensils, including tongs, lifter and brush are all essential—in fact, some people like to have two of each, to avoid cross-contamination. This means that you don't have to be constantly washing up your equipment whilst trying to cook. Avoid using forks as they have a tendency to pierce the meat, allowing the juices to escape.

THERMOMETER Some grills come with a thermometer, which is useful both for determining the temperature of the grill as well as the internal temperature of whatever you are cooking. If yours doesn't have one, invest in a meat thermometer which can serve both purposes—they're inexpensive and will save a lot of headaches. A few recipes in this book require a thermometer of some kind to monitor the cooking temperature over a long period—this is essential to avoid ending up with tough, overcooked meat.

A CHARCOAL STARTER CHIMNEY is another great bit of kit—put the chimney on the charcoal grate, fill with charcoal and put newspaper or firelighters underneath. Light the paper or firelighters and come back 15 minutes later. Pour the hot coals onto the cooking grate and away you go. You'll l also need foil drip pans if you plan to do a lot of indirect cooking. These are also useful for cooking meat in sauces and marinades over an indirect heat.

PLASTIC CONTAINERS with airtight lids, in various sizes, are useful for storing sauces and for marinating. Large re-sealable bags are also great for marinating—keep a few sizes on hand. Aluminum foil is a must—try cooking fish or delicate vegetables on a double layer of foil on the grill. It keeps fish from sticking without stopping it from browning.

barbecue has air vents below, open these up fully. If using a kettle barbecue, open the vents in the lid also. To reduce the heat, close the vents in the lid if you have them, or in the base if not.

If your food needs longer than 30 minutes, you'll need to cook it indirectly to avoid burning it. Kettle barbecues are particularly easy to use for indirect cooking, as they often come equipped with dividers just for the purpose. In any case, your barbecue will need to have a lid in order for you to cook indirectly. Install the dividers according the manufacturer's instructions and light separate fires in each, following the directions above.

If your barbecue doesn't have dividers, light the fire in the center as above, and then bank the coals either side to leave a space in the center of the cooking grate with no coals underneath. You can add a drip pan to the empty space below then replace the cooking grate. If cooking for longer than 1–1½ hours, you will probably need to add more coals to the fire. Add only a few at a time and allow these to catch and become covered in ash before adding more or you will lower the temperature and slow down the cooking.

If you have a gas grill, cooking directly simply means lighting all the burners and cooking anywhere on the grill. To cook indirectly, you need to extinguish one or more of the burners, then cook over these with the lid closed. Depending on the configuration of your grill, you may have to turn the meat more often than specified in the recipe—consult the manufacturer's instructions, if in doubt.

Direct-indirect?

All the recipes in this book specify whether the cooking should be done directly or indirectly. The temperatures indicated are easy to set for gas grills, but charcoal grills can be adjusted too. Generally speaking, if your food will cook in less than 30 minutes, cook it directly.

If you're using a charcoal barbecue, read the recipe to check how long you'll need to preheat your grill. For direct cooking, light the charcoal by putting a layer of coals or briquets onto the grate. Dot a few firelighters amongst the coals and light them using a long match. Carefully add another layer or two of coals or briquets until you have a very rough cone shape of coals or briquets. Allow the firelighters to burn down, then leave the coals until they are no longer flaming, but glowing red and covered in grey ash. This will take around 20–30 minutes. Again using tongs, spread the coals out to a larger area so that they are about two coals or briquets deep. Add the cooking grate, wait about 10 minutes for the grill to become hot, and you're ready to cook directly. If your

Cleaning your barbecue

Follow the manufacturer's instructions for cleaning the main body and lid of the barbecue.

For the cooking grate, it's best to clean it every time you use it. You don't need to scrub it until it shines, but it's best to remove any baked on bits from the last time you used it, otherwise they will add unwanted flavors to whatever you are cooking. Use a purpose-made metal brush to remove any large bits and then rub with a wire wool brush (they usually come together in one handy piece of equipment). The heat of the fire will kill off any bacteria that might still be lurking —another reason to add your cooking grate at least ten minutes before adding your food.

Is it done yet?

Most of the recipes in this book give a cooking time, but grilling, especially charcoal grilling, is an imprecise business and timings should be taken as a guideline. Recipes also provide an extra hint, such as 'until golden and heated through'. If in doubt, cut the food open and check that it is done to your taste. Do not be tempted to overcook meat in an effort to make it fall off the bone. This in itself does not necessarily indicate tenderness but can indicate meat that is dry and tough. Start checking the meat at the shortest suggested cooking time.

Burnt food is bad food

Flare-ups are the most common source of difficulty for the grill cook. Fire will burn your food, rather than cook it, giving it a very nasty flavor. Flare-ups are caused by fat dripping onto the coals or gas which then simply catches fire. To avoid excessive flare-ups, minimize the amount of oil you use in marinades, keep a very close eye on fatty foods like lamb and salmon, and keep the grill covered if possible—less oxygen means less fire. As a last resort, keep a spray bottle of water handy, but be careful because too much water can reduce the temperature of a charcoal fire and can also spray ashes onto your food.

As a general rule, it's a good idea to have a large container of water or the garden hose nearby—you never know, and it doesn't hurt to be prepared.

HOT! HOT! HOT!

If you want your recipes to have that truly authentic 'jump-in-your mouth' hot and spicy flavor, you'll need to become familiar with the wonderful world of chilies. So, don't be shy—get out there and explore! First off, take a look at the shelves of your nearest major supermarket—you'll be surprised at how many chili varieties are available there. You'll also find plenty in Asian, Hispanic and other ethnic grocery stores—so why not give them a visit, and see what they have on offer? Pretty soon you'll find that you're establishing your own preferences from the array of 'mild', 'medium', 'hot' and 'scorching' types that are on sale. Chilies are also available dried-whole, crushed or flaked in jars, and in paste form—so there's truly plenty of choice.

Apart from the specialist chilies mentioned below, many of the recipes featured in this book simply ask for a common red or green chili—keep a look-out for the most popular varieties such as Cascabel, Bird's eye and Serrano that are widely available at supermarkets. Chilies vary considerably in their flavors and levels of 'heat' so there's plenty of scope to experiment, and find which ones you like best. As a rule of thumb, the smaller the chili, the hotter it is.

Sometimes, for the best results, a recipe will call for a particular kind of chili; these are described here, on a scale that ranges from mild to positively scorching!

Mild

ANCHO This is the ripe, dry form of the poblano chili (see below). It is dark red-brown with wrinkled skin and adds a distinctive, fruity flavor to dishes.

ANAHEIM These are slender chilies, 6 inches (15cm) long, and may be red or green in color. They have a pure, sweet, earthy flavor and are great for stuffing.

GUAJILLO Guajillo is 4-6 inches (5–15cm) long and has a noticeably sweet flavor with a hint of wild berry. They are often sold dried and flaked as 'caribe'.

Medium

CHIPOTLE The chipotle is a ripened, dried and smoked jalapeño chili (see below). It is a light coffee color and has a superb, smoky, natural flavor.

POBLANO Fresh poblanos are dark green, wedge-shaped chilies, about 5–6 inches (13–15cm) long, that can range in heat from medium to fiery. They have a wonderfully complex flavor and are highly prized in Mexico. In their dried form they are called Anchos (see above).

Hot stuff!

The reason chilies are hot is because they contain a volatile oil called capsaicin. The first official method for defining its different strength levels in chilies was established in 1912 by Wilbur Scoville. This was overtaken by modern scientific techniques in 1980, but the levels are still coded in Scoville units. You often see this on the packaging or jar labels—chilies are rated from the lowest factor (1) to the highest (10)—so you'll have a good idea of how hot they are.

Handle with care

Capsaicin tends to be highly concentrated in the seeds and surrounding pith, which often needs to be removed and discarded. It's a good idea to wear rubber gloves when doing so—use your fingers or a knife to cut away the pith and remove the seeds. Don't forget, you should never touch your eyes or other sensitive places on the body when working with chilies, fresh or dried. The oil can be intensely irritating and painful. If you do use bare fingers, make sure that you wash your hands after you have finished working.

Hot

ARBOL This bright-to-deep red chili is 2–3 inches (5–7.5cm) long—and gives a bright, grassy flavor to dishes.

JALAPEÑO The Jalapeño is a smooth, dark-green pepper with a rounded tip, and can range in its heat intensity from hot to very hot!

PASILLO The pasillo chili is about 6 inches (15cm) long and has an deep, smoky, raisin flavor.

HABANERO (SCOTCH BONNET) The habanero chili can be green, red or yellow, and is prettily shaped like a tiny lantern. It the hottest chili in existence! Used sparingly, this will add a sharp, clean, citrus flavor to your recipes.

SMOKE GETS IN YOUR EYES

Smoking and flavoring

Cooking over wood can impart the most delicious range of flavors to barbecued food, so it's important for all good barbecue cooks to know how to exploit this possibility to the full. Smoking wood is available in various forms—as wood chips, which are suitable for food with shorter cooking times, and larger chunks for foods that take longer.

Wood chips can be used in a wood-burning pit, wood-burning grill or even a gas grill. To use them in a pit, grill or a gas grill unit, you need a cast-iron smoker box (otherwise use a heavy-duty aluminum foil container) to keep them from burning up. Soak them in water or apple juice for at least one hour before using.

The best way to smoke food is on a covered barbecue, but you can also scatter the wood among the coals of an open fire. Then, once it's burning well, you can damp it down with a little extra water to create more smoke.

If you're using chunks of wood, soak them for an hour before using and make sure they fit your barbecue pit. If you use two or three sticks about 7–15inches (17.5–35cm) long, and let them burn down to a bed of non-flaming coals, they should give you good results and provide a steady, source of heat and smoke.

When the wood starts smoking, begin grilling, and, if you're using a covered barbecue, keep the lid on. Add more soaked chips when you no longer see smoke coming out of the vents. Try not to overdo the smoking though; you want the flavor to enhance your food, not to overpower it.

CAUTION never use evergreen wood such as pine or spruce for smoking, as your food will be saturated with resins. Only use hardwoods for smoking and grilling.

The best woods to use for flavoring

BEEF Hickory, oak, mesquite
PORK Alder, pecan, cherry, hickory, maple and mesquite
LAMB Apple, cherry and oak
POULTRY Alder, apple, cherry, hickory, maple, mesquite and oak
FISH & SHELLFISH Alder, hickory, mesquite and oak

Wood flavors

OAK Excellent for smoking large pieces of meat such as brisket for considerable lengths of time, oak generally produces a medium to heavy (but not overpowering) flavor.
HICKORY Known as the king of woods, this will give food a strong, sweet, hearty flavor, and is perfect for ribs and pork shoulders.
PECAN This imparts a medium-fruity flavor—and is good for briskets and pork roasts.
APPLE Mild enough for chicken and turkey, apple has a mild, fruity flavor that makes meat taste slightly sweet. You could also use it to smoke a ham.
ALDER With its light, delicate, mild flavor, alder is perfect for cooking poultry and is also the traditional wood to choose for smoking salmon.
CHERRY Similar in flavor to apple, cherry has a mild, sweet, fruity flavor. It is extremely versatile, and you can use it for lamb, pork, ham, chicken and turkey.
MAPLE Mildly smoky, this goes well with poultry, ham and vegetables, imparting a sweet and light taste.
MESQUITE The flavor is strong and quickly transferred, so use this wood sparingly. The smoke should not penetrate the meat.

Smoke signals

Smoke is not only useful for cooking—it has a historic role in outdoor communication. Native American Indians used smoke signals to 'talk' to each other in secret code over great distances.

Some smoke signals now have a clear universal meaning for all woodsmen, plainsmen, and outdoor people, however. One puff means "pay attention" and two means "all's well". But three puffs indicates danger, trouble, or is a call for help. The signal should never be used as a joke, only as a genuine distress call.

birds
of a feather

OUR FEATHERED FRIENDS

Plump, tender poultry of all kinds are just great for the barbecue. These birds are a favorite with most folk, and their meat grills up moist and delicious.

Supermarkets and butchers carry a wide range of birds, which vary in quality and flavor according to the method of raising. You'll find labels covering various types: intensively reared (broiling) hens—often simply labeled 'fresh'; free range; and organic. They're easily accessible too: chicken and other poultry birds are available either fresh or frozen. However, quality does vary, so do a little research to decide which you are happiest buying.

Most supermarket chickens are broiling hens, which have been bred for their meat rather than for egg production. Also available are Cornish hens (poussins, or spring chickens). These are very young chickens—adolescents, if you like.

Look for a bird with plump, even-sized breasts and legs. Unwrap it when you get it home and dry it carefully with kitchen paper. If the bird comes with giblets, remove these immediately and either use them to make stock or freeze them for another time.

Chicken can be spiced up a treat with a dazzling variety of flavors, particularly fresh herbs of all types such as garlic, lemon, chilies, cilantro (coriander), tomatoes and all kinds of spices. It is truly the most versatile of all meats.

All cuts of chicken are suitable for barbecuing. Chickens can be cooked whole, rubbed with spices or jointed and cooked in pieces. Try stuffing a whole chicken with half an onion, a halved lemon and a handful of fresh herbs. Rub the skin with salt and pepper and cook over indirect heat for 1½ hours until golden and tender. Even quicker, butterfly a whole chicken and cook it over direct heat, turning often for 30–35 minutes—marinate the bird first for even more flavor.

Chicken pieces are infinitely versatile. Marinated in yogurt with spices, chicken legs are then grilled until golden and tender. Rub chicken breasts with roasted ground spices and serve with a hot and spicy barbecue sauce. Chicken wings musn't be overlooked, either—tossed in flour and spices, they come up tender and succulent, with a crispy skin, perfect for dipping in a creamy blue cheese sauce. And if you like turkey sandwiches you'll really love the apple and ginger marinated turkey steaks featured here.

Well! If you always thought that poultry was a bit predictable and unexciting, try some of these spicy little numbers—they'll transform an everyday bird into something really special.

Did we say turkey on the barbecue? You bet—it's really delicious cooked on the grill—and it's an ideal way to cook your Thanksgiving and Christmas bird. Barbecue a whole turkey indirectly over a medium-low heat—the bird will cook faster, and will therefore be less dry, than when it's roasted in the oven. And think of the oven space you'll have freed up for cooking all those accompaniments. Don't try to barbecue a bird that is any heavier than about 12 lbs/5.5kg though.

Grill-roasted spice-rubbed whole chicken

Delicious on its own served with potatoes and salad, this chicken also makes an excellent ingredient in other dishes that require cooked chicken, like the enchiladas recipe (page 20).

Serves 4

2 tbsp fennel seeds
1 tbsp coriander seeds
1 tbsp black peppercorns
1$^{1}/_{2}$ tsp chili flakes
2 tsp cayenne
2 tbsp salt
1 tsp ground cinnamon
3lb/ 1.5kg whole chicken

1 Preheat the barbecue grill to medium indirect heat.

2 Meanwhile, heat a small, dry, frying pan on the stove over medium heat and add the fennel seeds, coriander seeds, and black peppercorns. Cook for 1–2 minutes, shaking the pan often, until the spices smell aromatic and begin to brown. If you have an extractor fan, switch it on full, if not, open the window and add the chili flakes to the pan. Stand back to avoid the fumes and shake the pan for about 30 seconds. Remove the pan from the heat and quickly transfer the mixture to a plate to cool.

3 When the mixture is cool, transfer to a mortar and pestle or spice grinder and grind to a fine powder. Stir in the cayenne, salt, and cinnamon.

4 Wash the chicken inside and out and dry thoroughly with paper towel. Sprinkle about 2 tbsp

COOK'S TIP

The roasted spices in this recipe make 6 tbsp of mixture—more than you will need for this dish. Set aside the remainder in an airtight container and keep for future use.

of the spice mixture inside the chicken and all over the skin, rubbing it in well. If you have time, set aside to marinate for 30 minutes or more.

5 Cook the chicken over indirect medium heat for 1 hour, 20 minutes, or until golden and the juices run clear. The legs should pull away from the body easily—if they don't, give the chicken a further 10 minutes then try again.

6 Remove from the barbecue and let rest for 10 minutes before carving. Otherwise, leave until cold and carve or tear the meat from the bones to use in another recipe.

VARIATION
Grill-roasted chicken with spicy, smoky gravy

Put a foil tray under the cooking grate (between the coals in a kettle barbecue) filled with about 1 cup/250ml water. The tray will catch the juices from the chicken as it cooks. While the cooked chicken is resting, carefully remove the foil tray and transfer it to a roasting pan that will go on the stove (hob). Add ½ cup/125ml red or white wine and place over a high heat. Stir well to scrape up any deposits on the bottom of the foil tray. Add 1 cup/250ml chicken stock and bring to a boil. Simmer for about 5 minutes or until reduced by one third. Taste for seasoning. If you prefer a thicker gravy, mix 1 tbsp flour with 2 tbsp water to a smooth paste. Whisk this mixture, a little at a time, into the gravy, whisking constantly, until the gravy reaches the desired thickness. Simmer for a further 2 minutes, then serve.

Spicy chicken enchiladas

Serves 4

Here's a great way of using leftover barbecued chicken. The ready-prepared mole sauce, is enhanced with a little peanut butter to make a smoother sauce.

2 x 6fl oz/185ml jars prepared mole
  poblano paste
3 tbsp peanut butter
1 cup/250ml chicken stock
8 x 8 inch/20cm corn tortillas
3 cups/450g cooked, shredded Grill-roasted,
  Spice-rubbed Whole Chicken (page 18)
1 small onion, finely chopped
2½ cups/300g grated Cheddar or
  Monterey Jack cheese
  salt and freshly
  ground black
  pepper

To serve

crème fraîche or sour cream
  Pot Beans or Refried Beans (pages 126-7)
  Pico de Gallo (page 21)

1 Preheat the barbecue grill to medium indirect heat.

2 In a medium saucepan, mix together the mole poblano paste and peanut butter over a low heat. Mash together until melted. Gradually add enough of the chicken stock to make a smooth, thick sauce.

3 Warm the corn tortillas by wrapping them in aluminum foil and putting them on the barbecue for 3–4 minutes.

4 Spread about a quarter of the mole sauce in the bottom of a large size aluminum foil tray (13 x 8 inches/33 x 20cm). Lay one tortilla on a plate and top with about ⅓ cup/50g shredded chicken. Season lightly with salt and pepper and sprinkle over a little of the onion, then some of the cheese. Roll up and place, seam-side-down, in the aluminum foil tray. Repeat with the remaining tortillas and filling ingredients, reserving about ½ cup/55g of the cheese.

5 Spoon the remaining mole sauce over the enchiladas and sprinkle with the reserved cheese. Cover the tray loosely with aluminum foil and transfer to the barbecue.

6 Cook for 15 minutes until the enchiladas are heated through and the sauce is bubbling.

7 Transfer the enchiladas to serving plates and drizzle each with a little of the crème fraîche or sour cream. Serve immediately with a spoonful of pot beans or refried beans and pico de gallo.

Chili fajitas on the grill

Serves 4

This recipe takes a little preparation but is well worth the effort. Don't forget to save any leftover pico de gallo and guacamole to go with other dishes.

4 skinless, boneless chicken breasts
salt and freshly ground black pepper
8 x 8 inch/20cm flour tortillas, to serve

marinade
1 cup/250g ready-made tomato salsa
1 small red onion, roughly chopped
4 tbsp chopped fresh cilantro (coriander)
2 jalapeño chilies, seeded and
* roughly chopped*
2½ tsp tequila
juice of 2 limes
½ cup/125ml lager

pico de gallo
1lb/450g ripe tomatoes, seeded and diced
1 medium onion, finely chopped
4 tbsp chopped fresh cilantro (coriander)
2–3 fresh jalapeño chilies, seeded and
* finely chopped*
juice of 1 lime

guacamole
2 ripe avocados, Hass, if possible
2 plum tomatoes, seeded and diced
1 garlic clove, crushed
3 green (spring) onions, finely chopped
juice of 1 lemon
3 tbsp sour cream, plus extra to serve

1 Preheat the barbecue grill to medium direct heat.

2 In a blender or food processor, put the salsa, onion, cilantro (coriander), and chilies. Process until finely chopped before adding the tequila, lime juice, and lager. Process again briefly to mix.

3 Put the chicken breasts in a single layer in a non-metallic dish. Pour the marinade over and let stand for about 2 hours.

4 Meanwhile, for the pico de gallo, mix together the tomatoes, onion, cilantro (coriander), chilies, and lime juice. Season to taste, cover, and set aside until needed.

5 For the guacamole, cut the avocados in half lengthwise and remove the stone. Peel and roughly chop the flesh, then mash coarsely in a mixing bowl. Add the tomatoes, garlic, green (spring) onions, lemon juice, and sour cream. Season to taste, cover, and set aside until needed.

6 Lift the chicken from the marinade and cook over direct medium heat for 10–12 minutes, basting often with the marinade and turning once, until golden and cooked through. Remove from the barbecue and let rest for 10 minutes.

7 Meanwhile, wrap the tortillas in aluminum foil and warm on the barbecue for 3–4 minutes.

8 Slice the chicken breast thickly and arrange on a serving dish. Serve with the warmed tortillas, pico de gallo, guacamole and extra sour cream.

Grilled chicken breast in creamy ancho chilli sauce

Chilies are so popular they even have their own competitions and the judges award prizes in the categories of heat and flavor (see below). In this recipe, a chili called ancho is used.

Serves 4

It is the dried form of the fresh poblano chili, and has a sweet fruity flavor with a touch of tobacco. If you can get the fresh variety, however, you can substitute it for the dried ancho here. Serve this dish with Texas Pilaf (page 136).

4 boneless chicken breasts

cumin-oregano rub
1 tsp cumin seeds
½ tsp Mexican oregano
½ tsp salt

creamy ancho chili sauce
1 dried ancho chili
about 1 cup/250ml boiling water
2 tbsp olive oil
1 small onion, finely chopped
1 garlic clove, crushed
2 plum tomatoes, skinned, seeded, and chopped
½ cup/125ml chicken stock
¼ cup/60g cream cheese
2 tbsp chopped fresh cilantro (coriander)
salt and freshly ground black pepper

1 Preheat the barbecue grill to medium direct heat.

2 To make the creamy ancho chili sauce, put the ancho chili into a small bowl and cover with the boiling water. Let stand for 20 minutes until softened and swelled. Remove the stem and seeds and chop finely. Set aside until needed.

3 In a medium saucepan, heat the oil over medium heat. Add the onion and cook for 5–7 minutes until softened. Add the garlic and cook for a further minute. Add the tomatoes and cook for 2–3 minutes until softened before adding the chopped chili.

4 Stir in the chicken stock and bring to a boil. Simmer, covered, for 10 minutes. Add the cream cheese and stir until melted and the sauce has thickened. Add the cilantro (coriander) and season to taste.

5 Meanwhile, heat a small dry frying pan and add the cumin seeds. Cook over a medium heat for 3–4 minutes or until the seeds darken and become aromatic. Remove from the heat and let cool. Grind finely and mix with the oregano and salt.

6 Lay the chicken breasts on a chopping board and sprinkle the cumin mixture over. Rub in well on all sides.

7 Cook the chicken breasts over medium direct heat, skin-side-down first, for 12–15 minutes, turning once, until golden and cooked through, and the juices run clear.

8 Remove from the barbecue and let rest for 5 minutes before serving with the sauce.

'Dancing' chicken

Here, a whole chicken is cooked on a beer can, which is even better than a vertical roaster because the simmering spiced beer keeps the chicken moist, as well as adding flavor. Serve with **Coleslaw (page 138)** and **Spicy Grilled Potato Wedges (page 133)**.

3 lb/1.5kg whole chicken
1 quantity spice rub of your choice, such as that in Grill-roasted, Spice-rubbed Whole Chicken (page 18) or Grilled Chicken Breast in Creamy Ancho Chili Sauce (page 22)
12oz/330cl can of beer
salt and freshly ground black pepper

Serves 4

1 Wash the chicken, then dry thoroughly with paper towel. Rub inside and out with the spice rub. Set aside for 60 minutes.

2 Preheat the barbecue grill to medium indirect heat.

3 Pour out and drink about half the beer from the can. Add the remaining spice rub to the can. Stand the can in the center of a aluminum foil pan large enough to hold the chicken comfortably. Put the chicken over the can so that it rests on its legs. Now you can see why this is called Dancing Chicken!

4 Carefully transfer the foil tray to the barbecue and cook over medium indirect heat for 1 hour, 30 minutes, or until the bird is golden and the juices run clear.

5 Remove from the heat and let stand for 10 minutes, then carve and serve immediately.

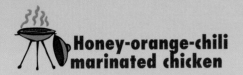

Honey-orange-chili marinated chicken

Serve this deliciously crispy-skinned chicken with Grilled Corn Cobs (page 131), Spiced Grilled Sweet Potatoes (page 130), and Homemade Mayonnaise (page 141).

3lb/1.5 kg whole chicken
juice of 2 oranges (about ¾ cup/185ml)
3 garlic cloves, crushed
5 tbsp runny honey
1 tbsp chopped chipotles in adobo
salt and freshly ground black pepper

1 Stand the chicken on a chopping board with its tail end upwards. Using a large, sharp knife or poultry shears, cut down one side of the backbone. Repeat down the other side of the backbone and remove it.

2 Lay the chicken, skin-side-up, and press down to crack the breastbone and flatten the bird.

3 In a large, non-metallic dish large enough to hold the bird, mix together the orange juice, garlic, honey, and chipotles in adobo. Add the chicken, skin-side-down, and let marinate for about 1 hour.

4 Preheat the barbecue grill to medium direct heat.

5 Wrap 2 average-size bricks in a double thickness of aluminum foil. Put the chicken, skin-side-down, on the barbecue grill and top with a baking sheet. Put the bricks on top of the baking sheet.

6 Grill for 5 minutes, then remove the baking sheet and bricks and turn the chicken. Brush with any remaining marinade. Replace the baking sheet and bricks. Keep removing the bricks and turning every 5–10 minutes, brushing with the marinade, until a total cooking time of about 35 minutes, ending skin-side-down. The chicken should be golden and the skin very crisp. The juices should run clear.

7 Transfer the chicken to a clean chopping board and cut in half through the breastbone. Remove the leg quarters and separate the drumsticks from the thighs. Cut the breasts in half crosswise to give 8 pieces. Serve immediately.

Serves 4

Spicy tequila-lime marinated chicken skewers with avocado salsa

2 large skinless, boneless chicken breasts,
  cut into 1½ inch/4cm chunks
¼ cup/60ml tequila
½ cup/125ml lime juice (about 4–5 limes)
2 garlic cloves
1 tbsp dried jalapeño chili flakes
2 tsp sugar
2 tbsp olive oil
16 cherry tomatoes
salt and freshly ground black pepper

avocado salsa
1 large avocado
1 garlic clove, crushed
1 plum tomato, seeded and diced

Serves 4

These tasty little chicken skewers make great appetizers. To serve as a main course, double the quantity of chicken and salsa and use large tortillas—you won't need to double the marinade.

½ small red onion, finely chopped
juice of 1 lime
1 tbsp chopped fresh cilantro (coriander)
  or parsley

to serve
sour cream
8 x 6 inch/ 15cm flour tortillas

1 In a non-metallic dish, mix together the tequila, lime juice, garlic, jalapeño flakes, sugar, and oil until the sugar has dissolved. Season with black pepper.

2 Add the chicken pieces and mix thoroughly to coat. Cover and set aside for at least 1 hour.

3 Meanwhile, cut the avocado in half lengthwise and carefully remove the stone. Finely dice the flesh and mix with the garlic, tomato, red onion, lime juice, and cilantro (coriander). Season to taste, cover and set aside until needed.

4 Preheat the barbecue to high direct heat.

5 Thread the chicken onto 8 metal or wooden skewers, putting a cherry tomato at either end of each skewer.

6 Cook the chicken skewers for 8–10 minutes, turning 2–3 times until golden and cooked, and the juices run clear. Meanwhile, wrap the tortillas in aluminum foil and heat through on the barbecue for 3–4 minutes.

7 Remove the skewers from the barbecue and serve immediately with the salsa, sour cream and tortillas.

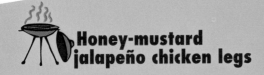

Honey-mustard jalapeño chicken legs

Like it really hot? In that case, increase the number of chilies in this recipe to three!

1 garlic clove, crushed
1 jalapeño chili, seeded and finely chopped
3 tbsp runny honey
2 tbsp Dijon mustard
juice of 1 lime (about 2 tbsp)
4 whole chicken legs
salt and freshly ground black pepper
lime wedges, to serve

1 Preheat the barbecue grill to medium direct heat.

2 In a small bowl, whisk together the garlic, chili, honey, mustard, and lime juice. Season to taste and set aside until needed.

3 Season the chicken legs with salt and pepper and cook, skin-side-down, for 25–30 minutes, turning once halfway through the cooking time until golden and the juices run clear. Brush liberally with the sauce during the last 5 minutes of cooking time.

Serves 4

Citrus-roasted chicken

This chicken looks really great when it is cooked, with the sliced citrus fruit and herbs showing through the skin—you might want to carve it at the table so everyone can admire it.

1 small orange, sliced
1 lemon, sliced
1 lime, sliced
2 cups/500ml water
4 tbsp sugar
3lb/1.5kg whole chicken
about 8–10 fresh basil leaves
3–4 sprigs fresh thyme
1 tbsp coriander seeds
1 tsp paprika
2 tbsp olive oil
salt and freshly ground black pepper

1 Put the orange, lemon, and lime slices with the water and sugar in medium saucepan over a low heat. Stir until the sugar has completely dissolved. Increase the heat and bring to a boil. Simmer for 10 minutes, remove from the heat and let cool.

2 Preheat the barbecue grill to medium indirect heat.

3 Working from the neck end, carefully loosen the skin of the chicken by working your fingers up underneath, taking care not to tear the skin. Continue to loosen the skin over the drumsticks as well.

Serves 4

4 When the skin is loose enough, carefully insert the cold orange, lemon, and lime slices under the skin over the drumsticks and breasts in an even layer. Add basil leaves and thyme sprigs as you go.

5 Heat a small dry frying pan and add the coriander seeds. Fry over a high heat until the seeds start to pop, then immediately remove from the heat to a mortar and pestle. Grind the seeds fairly finely. Add the paprika and mix together thoroughly.

6 Drizzle the oil over the chicken and rub evenly over the skin. Sprinkle the spice mixture evenly over the chicken. Season with salt and pepper and rub all the spices into the skin.

7 Cook over medium indirect heat for 1½ hours, until golden and tender and the juices run clear.

8 Remove from the heat and let rest for 10 minutes. Carve and serve immediately.

Cajun chicken breasts

Spice-rubbed chicken breasts are served with a hot Louisiana-style sauce.

Serves 4

4 bone-in chicken breasts with skin
salt and freshly ground black pepper

Louisiana-style sauce

3 tbsp peanut or other vegetable oil
1 large onion, finely chopped
1 celery stalk, finely chopped
1 small green bell pepper, finely chopped
3 tbsp chopped fresh parsley
2 garlic cloves, finely chopped
1/2 cup/125ml steak sauce
1–2 tsp Louisiana hot sauce or Tabasco
1/2 cup/125ml ketchup
1/4 cup/60ml Southern Comfort
1/2 cup/125ml chicken stock

spice-rub

2 1/2 tsp black peppercorns
1/2 tsp white peppercorns
1 1/2 tsp cumin seeds
1 1/2 tsp fennel seeds
1 tsp celery seeds
1 tsp salt
1 1/2 tsp paprika
1 tsp cayenne
1/2 tsp dried thyme

1 In a large saucepan, heat the oil and add the onion, celery, and bell pepper. Cook over a medium heat for 8–10 minutes until softened. Add the parsley and garlic and cook briefly before adding the remaining ingredients. Bring to a boil, reduce the heat and simmer very gently for about 2 hours until thickened. Stir often to keep the mixture from catching on the bottom of the pan. Season to taste and set aside until needed.

2 Make the spice-rub by putting all the whole spices into a spice grinder or mortar. Grind to a fine powder. Add the paprika, cayenne, and dried thyme and mix together well. Sprinkle the mixture over the chicken pieces and rub in well. Set aside to marinate for at least 30 minutes.

3 Preheat the barbecue grill to medium direct heat.

4 Cook the chicken breasts, skin-side-down, for 30–35 minutes until golden and tender, turning once halfway through the cooking time and basting with the sauce during the last 5 minutes of cooking time. Serve immediately.

Tandoori-style grill-roasted chicken legs

Traditionally, this dish is cooked in a tandoor, which is an urn-shaped clay oven that can reach very high temperatures. It is very difficult to recreate such high temperatures at home, but you can approximate the flavor by marinating the chicken in a spicy yogurt mixture and cooking on the barbecue.

Serves 4

1 tsp cumin seeds
2 tsp coriander seeds
2 tsp turmeric
1 tsp garam masala
1 tsp paprika
1 hot green chili, such as jalapeño, seeded
  and finely chopped
3 garlic cloves, crushed
2 tsp fresh ginger, finely grated
4 cups/500g plain (natural) yogurt
4 chicken legs, each cut in 2
salt and freshly ground black pepper

1 Heat a small dry frying pan over a high heat and add the cumin and coriander seeds. Cook for 1–2 minutes, until the seeds darken and begin to smell aromatic. Immediately remove from the heat and let cool. Grind as finely as possible and transfer to a mixing bowl along with the turmeric, garam masala, paprika, chili, garlic, and ginger. Add the yogurt and stir well to mix.

2 Using a sharp knife, cut slashes in the chicken pieces down to the bone. Add the chicken pieces to the yogurt mixture and mix well, using your hands to massage the yogurt mixture into the chicken. Cover and refrigerate for at least 6 hours and preferably overnight.

3 Preheat the barbecue to high direct heat. **4** Remove the chicken pieces from the marinade and brush off the excess. Cook, skin-side-down, for 20–25 minutes turning 2–3 times until golden and tender, and the juices run clear. Serve immediately.

Spice-rubbed turkey roast

Turkey is a jumbo-size bird, and requires long cooking. This can make the breast meat dry and overcooked before the rest of the bird has finished cooking through. To help prevent this, a spice-flavored butter is applied under the skin and the finished dish is served with a pineapple BBQ sauce.

Serves 4–6

2 tsp coriander seeds
1/2 cup/120g unsalted butter, softened
2 tsp fresh thyme
   leaves
peel and juice of
   1/2 orange
1 tsp dried red chili
   flakes
1 crown turkey,
   about 3–41/2 lb/
   1.5–1.75kg
salt and freshly
   ground black pepper

pineapple BBQ sauce

1 small onion, finely chopped
425g/15oz can crushed pineapple or
   pineapple pieces, drained and finely
   chopped
2 tbsp cider vinegar
1 tbsp Worcestershire sauce
3 tbsp dark soy sauce
1/2 cup/125ml ketchup
1 tsp Dijon mustard
pinch Chinese five-spice powder
1 tsp Tabasco or 1 dried ancho chili, seeded
   and chopped
1 tbsp molasses
1/2 lemon, thinly sliced, seeds removed

1 Preheat the barbecue grill to medium indirect heat.

2 Heat a small dry frying pan and when hot, add the coriander seeds. Cook for 1–2 minutes until the seeds darken and start to pop. Remove from the heat and let cool. Grind finely and set aside.

3 Put the butter into a small mixing bowl and add half the ground coriander seeds, thyme leaves, orange peel, and chili flakes. Mix together well, then add the orange juice and beat until smooth. Season to taste.

4 Loosen the skin over the breast of the turkey by working your hand carefully up and under the skin. Push the flavored butter under the skin to cover the breast evenly. Put the turkey into a aluminum foil tray big enough to hold it comfortably.

5 Season the turkey skin, then sprinkle the remaining coriander seeds over. Rub into the skin well until evenly covered.

6 Cook the turkey for 1½ hours until golden and tender, and the juices run clear. Let rest for 10 minutes.

7 Meanwhile, put all the sauce ingredients into a medium saucepan and bring to a boil. Simmer very gently for 1½ hours until the onion and lemon have softened.

8 Carve the turkey breast by removing each breast and then slicing. Serve with the sauce.

Apple and ginger marinated turkey breast sandwiches

These are great tasting, rustic, open-faced sandwiches. They are substantial enough to serve for supper, perhaps with some Spicy Grilled Potato Wedges (page 133) and a green salad.

4 turkey breast steaks
1 large onion, thickly sliced
1 tbsp olive oil
2 dessert apples, such as Granny Smith, cored and thickly sliced crosswise
salt and freshly ground black pepper
rocket leaves, to serve

apple marinade
½ cup/ 125ml apple juice, preferably cloudy
2 tbsp cider vinegar
2 tsp finely grated fresh ginger
1 garlic clove, crushed
3 cloves

Texas toast
6 tbsp butter, softened
1 garlic clove, crushed
4 thick slices rustic bread

herb and mustard mayonnaise
½ quantity Homemade Mayonnaise (page 141)
2 tsp wholegrain Dijon mustard
3 tbsp chopped fresh herbs, such as chives, basil, thyme, and mint

1 In a small saucepan, mix together the apple juice, vinegar, ginger, garlic, and cloves over a low heat. Bring to a boil and simmer for 2 minutes, then remove from the heat. Let cool.

2 Put the turkey steaks in a single layer into a non-metallic dish. Pour the cooled marinade over. Cover and marinate for at least 60 minutes.

3 Preheat the barbecue grill to high direct heat.

4 For the Texas toast, mix together the butter and garlic. Season with salt and pepper. Cover and set aside (not in the refrigerator) until needed.

5 Put the mayonnaise into a small mixing bowl and add the mustard and fresh herbs. Mix together well, cover and set aside until needed.

6 Brush the onion slices with the olive oil and cook over high direct heat for 10–12 minutes, turning often and carefully, until golden and tender.

7 Cook the apple slices alongside the onions for 4–5 minutes, turning often until golden and tender.

8 Lift the turkey steaks from the marinade, shaking off the excess. Cook, alongside the onion and apple slices, over high direct heat for 6–8 minutes, turning once halfway through the cooking time.

9 Meanwhile, toast the bread over high direct heat until golden on both sides. Remove from the heat and spread generously with the flavored butter.

10 Top the buttered toast with a turkey steak, some onion, 2 apple slices and a dollop of herb mayonnaise. Serve immediately with a few rocket leaves.

Serves 4

Butterflied margarita-marinated Cornish game hens

Cornish hens (poussins) are young chickens with a very delicate flavor. This marinade gives a real kick to the taste buds, and the butterflied birds look great too.

Serves 4

4 Cornish game hens (poussins),
  about 1lb/450g each
½ cup/125ml fresh lime juice
(about 4–5 limes)
⅓ cup/75ml gold tequila
¼ cup/60ml olive oil
2 tbsp orange liqueur or orange juice
2 garlic cloves, crushed
2 hot red chilies, seeded and
  finely chopped
salt and freshly ground black pepper
1 quantity Guacamole (page 21) to serve

1 Using a sharp knife or poultry shears, remove the backbone from each of the hens. Lay them skin-side-up and push down to crack the breastbone.

2 In a large, non-metallic dish, mix together the lime juice, tequila, olive oil, orange liqueur, garlic, and chili. Add the hens, turning to coat well and leaving them skin-side-down in the marinade. Leave to marinate for about 2 hours, turning once or twice.

3 Preheat the barbecue grill to medium indirect heat.

4 Remove the hens from their marinade, shaking off any excess. To butterfly the birds, push a metal or wooden skewer through the drumstick on one side and out through the wing on the other side. Repeat to have two crossed skewers through the bird holding it flat.

5 Season to taste and cook, skin-side-down, over medium indirect heat for 30–40 minutes, brushing with the marinade occasionally and turning 2–3 times until golden and tender, and the juices run clear. Remove the skewers and serve immediately or let cool and serve at room temperature with the guacamole.

Chili-rubbed Cornish game hens

You'll probably have some of the homemade chili paste from this recipe left over, but it keeps well and is a versatile flavor enhancer. Try stirring a spoonful into barbecue sauces or tomato sauces in place of fresh or dried chilies.

2oz/55g dried ancho chilies
1½ oz/40g dried guajillo chilies
2½ oz/65g dried chilies de arbol, stemmed, seeded and roughly chopped
about 3 cups/750ml boiling water
4 Cornish game hens (poussins), about 1lb/450g each
6 tbsp unsalted butter, softened
1¾lb/750g small new potatoes
4oz/115g fine green beans, trimmed
½ quantity Mayonnaise (page 141)
peel and juice of 1 lemon
1 tsp coarsely cracked black peppercorns
2 green (spring) onions, finely chopped
salt

1 Preheat the barbecue to medium indirect heat.

2 Heat a small dry frying pan, and when hot, add the ancho and guajillo chilies. Toast for 3–4 minutes until softened and fragrant. Let cool, then remove stems and seeds and chop coarsely. Put into a medium mixing bowl with the chilies de arbol.

3 Pour the boiling water over the chilies and stir well. Let stand for about 1 hour (longer, if possible) until they are soft. Drain, reserving about 2–3 tbsp of the soaking water.

4 Put the chilies into a food processor or blender. Process to chop finely, adding a little of the reserved soaking water until you have a purée. Take care not to add too much water—you want to end up with a thick mixture. Transfer to a sieve and press through into a bowl. Discard any seeds or tough bits left in the sieve. This will make about 2/3 cup/200ml of chili purée.

5 Loosen the skin of the Cornish hens, starting at the neck end, by working your fingers carefully up underneath, taking care not to tear the skin. In a small bowl, mix together the butter with 3 tbsp of the chili purée.

6 Push about 1 tbsp of the chili mixture up under the skin evenly over the breast and drumsticks. Season to taste.

7 Cook the birds over medium indirect heat for 50–60 minutes until golden and tender, and the juices run clear. Remove from the heat and let rest for 10 minutes.

8 Meanwhile, boil the new potatoes for 12–15 minutes until tender, adding the beans during the last 4 minutes. Drain well and run under cold running water. Drain well again and set aside.

9 Put the mayonnaise into a large mixing bowl and add the lemon peel, juice and black pepper. Stir in the cooked potatoes and beans along with the green (spring) onions. Serve with the Cornish hens.

COOK'S TIP
Any leftover chili purée can be frozen in ice cube trays, then stored in freezer bags for up to 2 months.

Wings with hot and spicy Mexican adobo barbecue sauce

Use this classic fiery barbecue sauce with a variety of grilled meats, as well as these tasty wings. This recipe makes more than you need, so you can freeze any leftover amount for up to 3 months.

1 small garlic bulb
2 tsp dry sherry
1 tbsp olive oil
1 sprig fresh thyme
1lb/450g plum tomatoes
1/2 small onion, finely chopped
3 tbsp caribe (dried chili flakes)
1/4 cup/60ml sherry or white wine vinegar
1/2 tsp dried Mexican oregano
1/2 tsp ground cumin
pinch dried thyme
pinch mixed spice
2 tbsp brown sugar
2 tsp salt
freshly ground black pepper
1/2 cup/125ml fresh orange juice
3lb/1.5kg chicken wings

1 Preheat the oven to 400°F/200°C, gas 6. Pull away the very papery skin from the garlic and cut the top third off to expose the garlic cloves. Wrap in aluminum foil without sealing and drizzle in the sherry and olive oil. Add the thyme sprig and seal well. Bake in the oven for about 1 hour until very tender. Squeeze all the garlic out of its skin and set aside.

2 Preheat the barbecue grill to medium direct heat.

3 Cook the tomatoes on the barbecue for about 6–8 minutes in their skins until blackened and slightly softened. Remove from the grill and chop coarsely without removing the skin.

4 Put the tomatoes, roasted garlic, onion, caribe, vinegar, oregano, cumin, thyme, mixed spice, and sugar into the bowl of a food processor or blender. Season to taste. Run the machine until the sauce is fairly smooth, scraping down the sides as necessary. Add the orange juice and pulse to mix to a smooth sauce.

5 Increase the barbecue heat to high. Cook the chicken wings for 30–35 minutes, turning 2–3 times until golden and the juices run clear. Baste with the sauce during the last 5 minutes of cooking to avoid burning it. Serve immediately.

Serves 6

Outdoor Grub: Hot & Spicy Barbecue

Buffalo-style hot spiced chicken wings with blue cheese dip

These are delicious crispy wings—serve them as an appetizer or even as a canapé. Make sure you provide napkins, as they have to be eaten with fingers.

3lb/ 1.5kg chicken wings
3 tbsp plain flour
1–2 tsp ground cayenne pepper, to taste
1 tsp paprika
1 tsp dried oregano
1 quantity Blue Cheese Mayonnaise (see
  Buffalo Burgers, page 117)
3 tbsp sour cream
1 tbsp lemon juice
salt and freshly ground black pepper
celery stalks, trimmed, to serve

1 Preheat the barbecue grill to medium direct heat.

2 Trim the wings by removing the wing tip. Cut them in half through the joint, if preferred.

3 Put the flour, cayenne pepper, paprika, oregano, and plenty of salt and pepper into a large, clear plastic bag (a freezer bag is ideal). Shake well to mix, then add the chicken wings. Close the bag tightly at the top and shake until all the wings are well coated in the flour mixture.

4 Transfer the wings to a chopping board or baking sheet, shaking off any excess flour back into the bag. Discard any unused mixture.

5 Put the blue cheese mayonnaise into a small mixing bowl and add the sour cream and lemon juice. Season to taste and set aside until needed.

6 Cook the wings over medium direct heat for 30–35minutes, turning often, until golden and crisp. Serve immediately with the dip and celery stalks.

BEEF: YOUR FIRST CHOICE FOR THE GRILL

There's nothing like a first class piece of beef cooked to perfection on the grill. It has such a fine flavor and texture, and it's also really versatile too.

The most important thing to look for when choosing beef is a good supplier. Supermarket beef is often sold before it is ready. Like game, beef needs to be hung before it is ready to be cooked. Good suppliers will hang beef for up to 3 weeks before butchering it. The meat will be dark, even mahogany-colored with a good rim of creamy yellow fat. Bright red meat with white fat may look superficially fine, but it will be tough and tasteless.

Unlike pork, beef has a distinctly strong flavor of its own, and needs really inventive taste partners. Some flavors that play well with beef are black pepper, tomatoes, cumin, lime, chilies and cilantro (coriander).

Brisket is a perennial barbecue favorite. When cooking a brisket, you'll find that a thermometer becomes a vital piece of equipment—cooked at too high a temperature, the meat will be dry and tough; but cook it at just the right temperature, and you'll have meltingly succulent meat that will cut easily with a fork. Brisket is great for serving a large crowd, that's why it's always sold in a large piece. Plan to serve it as a grand centerpiece for a festive occasion. Look for brisket on the bone—and avoid buying rolled brisket, which may be suitable for slow braising, but not for barbecuing.

Burgers are another barbecue favourite. This everyday dish becomes something truly special when properly grilled and spiced up. The cheeseburgers in this book require very little in the way of extra embellishment—serve them simply with toasted buns and mayonnaise—and don't forget a few spicy grilled potatoes. If you prefer a more traditional burger, mix the ground beef with a small grated onion, a crushed garlic clove and about a tablespoon of Worcestershire sauce. Season generously and shape as usual —and you have fantastic burgers to serve with all the trimmings.

Beef is a great choice when you're entertaining a crowd of people. Serve Salpicon, a delicious fiery beef salad, or Carne Asada, a mixed plate of Mexican-style specialities. Beef ribs served with a fabulous coffee barbecue sauce are unusual and impressive —if anything, they're even more succulent than pork ribs.

Black bean chili with Texas-rubbed grilled steak

This delicious black bean chili is simple to make and is a fine accompaniment to the spice-rubbed and barbecued steak. You will need to soak the dried beans the day before you intend to make the chili, which also tastes good if made in advance. Serve with Guacamole (page 21) and a spoonful of sour cream.

4 sirloin steaks or strip loins, about
6–8oz/175–225g each

spice-rub
1 tsp cumin seeds
1 tsp black peppercorns
1 tbsp hot or mild chili flakes, to taste
½ tsp soft brown sugar
½ tsp garlic powder (not salt)
½ tsp salt
freshly ground black pepper
2 tbsp chopped fresh cilantro (coriander)

chili
1 cup/250g dried black turtle
  beans or black kidney beans
3 tbsp olive oil
2 onions, chopped
2 garlic cloves, crushed
1–2 hot green chilies, to taste,
  seeded and finely chopped
2 tbsp mild or hot chili seasoning
1 tsp ground cumin
1 tsp paprika
2 x 14oz/400g cans chopped tomatoes
1 tsp dried oregano

1 Put the beans into a large bowl and cover with at least twice their volume of cold water. Let soak for 8 hours or overnight.

2 Next day, drain the beans and put into a large saucepan. Cover with fresh cold water and bring to a boil. Boil hard for 10 minutes, then reduce the heat and simmer for about 40 minutes, until the beans are tender. Drain well and set aside.

3 Heat the oil in a large saucepan. Add the onions and cook for 7–8 minutes, until softened and starting to brown. Add the garlic and chilies and cook for another minute. Add the chili seasoning, cumin, and paprika and cook for about 30 seconds before adding the tomatoes and oregano. Simmer the chili gently, uncovered, for 20 minutes. Add the beans, stir, and simmer for a further 30–40 minutes, uncovered, until the chili has thickened. Season to taste.

4 Meanwhile, heat a small dry frying pan and add the cumin seeds and black peppercorns. Cook over a high heat for 1–2 minutes, until the cumin seeds darken and become aromatic. If you have an extractor fan, switch it on to full or open a nearby window. Add the chili flakes to the pan and shake the pan for about 20–30 seconds, keeping your head away from the pan to avoid the chili fumes.

5 Transfer the mixture to a mortar and pestle or spice grinder and let cool, then grind to a fine powder. Add the soft brown sugar, garlic powder, and salt and mix together thoroughly.

6 Preheat the barbecue grill to high direct heat.

7 Rub the spice mixture evenly into the steaks on both sides. Cook over high direct heat for 8–10 minutes, turning once halfway through the cooking time.

8 Remove from the heat and let stand for 5 minutes. Slice the steak thickly and serve immediately on top of the chili with guacamole and sour cream, and some chopped fresh cilantro (coriander).

Pot Beans or Refried Beans (page 126)
1/2 quantity Chicken Enchiladas (page 20)
1 quantity Guacamole (see Chili Fajitas,
  page 21)
1 quantity Pico de Gallo
 (see Chilli Fajitas, page 21)
tortilla chips

1 In a shallow non-metallic dish, whisk together the lime juice, olive oil, and garlic, and season to taste. Add the steaks and turn to coat in the marinade. Set aside to marinate for about 1 hour, turning the steaks once or twice.

2 Preheat the barbecue grill to high direct heat.

Serves 6

3 Roast the chilies over high direct heat until evenly charred. Set aside in a plastic bag or covered bowl until cool enough to handle. Peel away the skin. Remove the stems and seeds, and slice the flesh into strips. Set aside.

4 Cook the steaks over high direct heat for about 8–10 minutes, depending on thickness, brushing with the marinade once or twice, until medium-rare. During the last 2–3 minutes of cooking, divide the chili strips between the steaks, then cover with cheese slices. The cheese should melt.

5 Remove from the heat and transfer to serving plates along with a spoonful of beans, an enchilada, some guacamole, pica de gallo, and a handful of tortilla chips. Serve immediately.

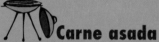

Carne asada

'Carne asada' literally means roasted meat, though the marinated steak is usually barbecued before being topped with roasted chilies. It is then served with classic accompaniments, such as enchiladas, beans or refried beans, guacamole, salsa, cheese, and tortilla chips. Delicious!

5 tbsp lime juice (about 1–2 limes)
1 1/2 tbsp olive oil
2 garlic cloves, crushed
6 skirt or fillet steaks, about 6oz/175g each
3 poblano chilies
salt and freshly ground black pepper

to serve
12oz/350g sliced Monterey Jack or
  Cheddar cheese

Hot & spicy cheeseburgers

These unusual hot and spicy burgers have the cheese inside them, instead of on top, so the mixture stays moist, even if you accidentally overcook them.

1lb/450g ground (minced) beef
½ cup/125g ready-made salsa
4oz/115g Cheddar or Monterey Jack cheese,
  cut into ½ inch/1cm cubes
1 garlic clove, crushed
salt and freshly ground black pepper

to serve
4 hamburger buns, sliced tomato, lettuce,
  relish, mustard, etc

1 Preheat the barbecue grill to high direct heat.

2 In a large bowl, mix together the ground (minced) beef, salsa, cheese, and garlic. Season generously with salt and pepper. Divide the mixture evenly into 4 and shape into disks about ¾ inch/2cm thick, prodding the cheese in so that it isn't on the surface.

3 Cook over high direct heat for 8–10 minutes, turning once halfway through the cooking time, until golden and cooked through.

4 Toast the buns on the barbecue for 1–2 minutes and serve with the burgers and accompaniments of your choice.

Serves 4

Salpicon

Serve this spectacular classic El Paso dish as the centerpiece of a buffet party. Unless you have a gas barbecue, you will need to be on hand to keep the fire stoked during the long cooking time.

Serves 6–8

5 cups/ 1.2lt canned beef consommé
3lb/ 1.5kg top-cut beef brisket
1 large onion, sliced
2 poblano chilies or 1 dried ancho chili
3 tbsp chipotles in adobo, puréed
3 tbsp olive oil
¼ cup/ 60ml lime juice (about 2 limes)
2 tbsp white wine vinegar
1 garlic clove, crushed
4oz/ 115g mild cheese, such as Cheddar or
  Monterey Jack, cut into small dice
1 red onion, roughly chopped
3 tbsp chopped fresh cilantro (coriander)
1 small head Romaine (Cos) lettuce, leaves
  washed and dried
3 medium tomatoes, cut into wedges
1 avocado, stoned and cut into wedges with
  skin on
salt
small corn or flour tortillas, to serve

1 Preheat barbecue grill to medium indirect heat.

2 In a saucepan, bring the consommé to a simmer, then set aside.

3 Put the brisket, fat-side-up, into a doubled foil tray. Scatter over the onion slices and transfer the tray to the barbecue. Pour in the hot beef consommé and add enough cold water to cover the meat completely. Cover loosely with foil or with another upturned foil tray.

4 Once the liquid starts to simmer, reduce the heat to low on a gas barbecue. Cook for 3–4 hours, turning the meat about halfway through the cooking time and adding additional boiling water as necessary. The meat should be tender enough to shred easily at its thickest point.

5 Carefully remove the tray from the barbecue and let the meat stand in its liquid until just cool enough to handle.

6 Meanwhile, if using fresh poblano chilies, roast them over the direct heat portion of the barbecue until evenly charred. Put into a plastic bag or covered bowl until cool enough to handle, then peel the skin. Remove the stems and seeds and finely slice the flesh. If using dried ancho chilies, soak in boiling water for about 20 minutes until softened and swelled. Remove the stems and seeds and slice the flesh finely.

7 Pour the broth from the meat and reserve about 1½ cups/375ml. Trim the fat from the brisket and using two forks, shred the meat as thoroughly as possible.

8 In a large bowl, mix together the shredded beef and reserved broth. Let stand at room temperature for at least 30 minutes and up to 2 hours.

9 Meanwhile, in a medium bowl, whisk together the chipotles in adobo, olive oil, lime juice, vinegar, and garlic, and season with salt to taste.

10 Drain the meat, pressing to remove as much stock as possible. Return the meat to the large bowl and add the chipotle mixture, cheese, red onion, cilantro (coriander), and sliced chili. Toss together well and taste for seasoning.

11 To serve, line a large platter with Romaine (Cos) leaves. Pile the meat mixture in the center. Arrange the tomatoes and avocado wedges (do not peel the avocado) around the meat. Serve with warmed tortillas.

Smoked slow-grilled brisket with Texas barbecue sauce

This recipe is technically indoor-outdoor grub, since the meat is finished in the oven. It can of course be entirely cooked on the barbecue, but the fire will require a lot of tending during that time to keep the temperature even and to prevent it from going out.

2 cups/500ml beef stock or broth, canned or homemade
1/4 cup/60ml Worcestershire sauce
2 tbsp dark brown sugar
2 tsp Tabasco
3 garlic cloves, crushed
5lb/2.25kg top-cut brisket

Texas barbecue sauce
1/2 cup/80g firmly packed brown sugar
2 tbsp chili seasoning
1 tbsp finely ground black pepper

Serves 6–8

1/2 onion, finely chopped
1 garlic clove, crushed
2 tsp celery salt
1/4–1/2 tsp cayenne (optional)
2 cups/500ml tomato ketchup
1/2 cup/125ml prepared mustard
1/4 cup/60ml cider vinegar
3 tbsp Worcestershire sauce
2 tsp liquid smoke (optional)
2 tbsp canola or vegetable oil

You will also need hickory smoking chips or chunks, soaked according to the packet instructions, then drained.

1 In a medium bowl, whisk together the stock or broth, Worcestershire sauce, brown sugar, Tabasco, and garlic. Transfer the marinade to a large re-sealable bag, then add the brisket. Seal the bag well and turn and knead it to coat the meat in the marinade. Set aside at room temperature for 1 hour.

Beer brisket

In this recipe, the brisket is partly cooked over a direct heat, while being coated with a flavorful beer mop. The meat is then transferred to a foil tray and cooked in the mop sauce. Serve with tortillas or place in crusty bread or rolls.

1 tbsp cumin seeds
2 tsp oregano
2 cups/500ml beer
5lb/2.25kg top-cut brisket
salt and freshly ground black pepper
tortillas or crusty bread or rolls, to serve

1 Heat a small dry frying pan and when hot, add the cumin seeds. Cook for 1–2 minutes, until the seeds darken and smell aromatic. Remove from the heat and transfer to a spice grinder or mortar and pestle. Let cool, then grind finely. Mix the cumin with the oregano, then season.

Serves 6–8

2 To make the barbecue sauce, combine all the ingredients except the oil in a medium saucepan. Bring to a boil, stirring to dissolve the sugar. (You may want to have a lid handy to protect yourself and kitchen from any sputtering.) Reduce the heat and simmer for 30 minutes, stirring often, until the onion has softened. With a whisk, blend in the oil until incorporated. Set aside until needed.

3 Preheat barbecue grill to medium indirect heat.

4 Add the smoking chips or chunks. Remove the meat from its marinade and lay on the center of the barbecue. Cover and cook for 2 hours, maintaining a temperature of about 230–275°F/120–140°C, gas ¼–1.

5 Meanwhile, preheat the oven to 350°F/180°C, gas 4. Transfer the brisket to a large piece of doubled aluminum foil. Pour the barbecue sauce over and seal tightly. Place in a foil tray or roasting pan and transfer to the oven. Bake for 2–3 hours, until very tender.

2 In a small jug or bowl, mix together the beer and the spice mixture and set aside.

3 Preheat the barbecue grill to medium indirect heat. In this case, you will need to bank the coals in a charcoal barbecue in such a way that the meat can be cooked over them to begin with, but with enough room to allow the meat to be cooked indirectly later. You may find it simplest to move the coals.

4 Put the meat over a direct heat and cook for 30 minutes, mopping with the beer mixture often and turning every 10 minutes or so.

5 Remove the meat from the barbecue and transfer to a large doubled foil tray or a large sheet of doubled aluminum foil. Pour the remaining beer mixture over and seal the parcel.

6 Remove from the oven and let stand, still sealed in foil, for 20 minutes. Transfer to a carving board and remove any obvious fat. Slice thickly across the grain and serve immediately with the sauce.

6 Transfer to the barbecue and cook over low indirect heat for 4 hours, checking and re-stoking the fire to maintain a temperature of 250–275°F/120–140°C, gas ½–1.

7 Remove from the barbecue when very tender and let stand in its packet for 20 minutes. Transfer to a carving board, discarding any juices and fat remaining in the foil. Remove any obvious fat and slice the meat thickly across the grain. Serve with tortillas or on crusty bread or rolls.

Beef ribs with coffee barbecue sauce

Beef ribs are less common than pork ribs, but are equally satisfying, if not more so. Definitely finger food—your guests will need fingerbowls and plenty of napkins.

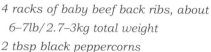

Serves 4

4 racks of baby beef back ribs, about 6–7lb/2.7–3kg total weight
2 tbsp black peppercorns
1 tbsp hot chili flakes
1 tbsp brown sugar
1/2 tsp garlic salt

coffee barbecue sauce

1 tbsp olive oil
1 medium red onion, finely chopped
1 clove garlic, finely chopped
11/2 tsp ground cumin
1 tsp oregano
1/2 tsp chili flakes
pinch ground cinnamon
1/2 cup/125ml chicken stock
4 tbsp ketchup
2 tbsp sherry vinegar
3 tbsp fresh orange juice
1/2 cup/80g packed brown sugar
11/2 tsp ground coffee

1 Preheat barbecue grill to medium indirect heat.

2 Wrap the racks of ribs individually in aluminum foil. Seal tightly. Cook the packets over medium indirect heat for about 1 hour, 30–40 minutes until tender. Cool in their packets

to room temperature. (You can cook them in the oven, if preferred, at 400°F/200°C, gas 6.)

3 Meanwhile, heat a small dry frying pan and when hot, add the black peppercorns. Cook for 1–2 minutes until aromatic. If you have an extractor fan, turn it on full or open a nearby window. Add the chili flakes to the pan and shake for about 15 seconds, keeping your head away

from the chili fumes. Transfer to a spice grinder or pestle and mortar and let cool. Grind to a coarse powder and stir in the brown sugar and garlic salt. Set aside.

4 Meanwhile, to make the coffee barbecue sauce, heat the oil in a medium saucepan. When hot, add the onion and garlic and cook for 5–7 minutes, until softened. Add the cumin, oregano, chili flakes, and cinnamon and cook for a further 30 seconds or so. Add the remaining ingredients and bring to a boil. Reduce the heat and simmer gently for about 20 minutes, until thickened.

5 Re-arrange the coals or ignite a gas barbecue as necessary to create a high direct heat.

6 Cut the ribs into smaller portions. Sprinkle generously with the black pepper mixture and pat to make sure it sticks. Cook over high direct heat for 12–15 minutes, turning often, until crisp and heated through. Brush with the sauce during the last 4–5 minutes of grilling.

7 Serve the ribs immediately with any remaining sauce.

Marinated and stuffed rib-eye steaks

Serves 4

Rib-eye steak is much underrated—it is full of flavor and delightfully moist. It doesn't need a lot of embellishment, so here it is simply stuffed with chilies and topped with garlic butter. Serve with grill-baked potatoes and a green salad.

4 dried ancho chilies
1 cup/250ml boiling water
3 garlic cloves, crushed
4 thick (about 1½ inch/4cm) rib-eye
  steaks, about 3lb/1.5kg total weight
salt and freshly ground black pepper

garlic and herb butter
½ cup/120g unsalted butter, softened
2 garlic cloves, crushed
1 tbsp fresh thyme leaves
1 tbsp chopped fresh chives
finely grated peel of ½ lemon

1 To make the garlic and herb butter, in a medium mixing bowl, beat the butter with the garlic, thyme, chives, and lemon peel. Season to taste. Scrape the mixture onto a large piece of waxed paper and, using the paper to help you, shape into a log about 1½in/4cm diameter. Seal the ends. Refrigerate until needed.

2 Put the ancho chilies into a bowl and cover with the boiling water (you may need a little more). Let soak for about 20 minutes until softened and swelled.

3 Preheat the barbecue grill to high direct heat.

4 Remove the stems and split the chilies open lengthwise to remove the seeds. Divide the garlic between the soaked chilies, spreading it inside each one and folding the chili back over so it is re-formed. Season to taste. Set aside until needed.

5 Using a small sharp knife, cut a horizontal pocket in each steak large enough to hold a chili. Put 1 chili in each pocket and press gently on the steak to close. Season to taste.

6 Cook the steaks over high direct heat for 6–10 minutes (6 minutes for rare), turning once halfway during cooking time.

7 Meanwhile, slice the garlic and herb butter thickly. Remove the steaks from the grill and put onto individual serving plates. Top each steak with 1 or 2 disks of butter and serve immediately.

Texas t-bones

T-bone steaks are always impressive. In this recipe, they are given the Texas treatment with a flavorful Southwestern spice-rub and then served with a barbecue-roasted tomato salsa.

4 small or 2 large T-bone steaks, about 3lb/1.5kg total weight

spice-rub
2 tsp cumin seeds
2 tsp black peppercorns
2 tbsp chili flakes, hot or mild, to taste
1 tsp brown sugar
1 tsp garlic powder (not salt)
1/2 tsp salt

roasted tomato salsa
6 plum tomatoes, halved
1 red onion, thickly sliced
4 tbsp olive oil
1 garlic clove, finely chopped
2 tsp sherry vinegar
2 tbsp chopped fresh parsley or cilantro (coriander)
salt and freshly ground black pepper

1 Preheat the barbecue grill to high direct heat.

2 Heat a small dry frying pan and add the cumin seeds and black peppercorns. Cook over a high heat for 1–2 minutes, until the cumin seeds darken and become aromatic. If you have an extractor fan, switch it on full or open a nearby window. Add the chili flakes and shake the pan for about 20–30 seconds, keeping your head away from the pan to avoid the chili fumes.

3 Transfer the mixture to a mortar and pestle or spice grinder and let cool, then grind to a fine powder. Add the brown sugar, garlic powder, and salt, and mix together thoroughly.

4 Rub the mixture evenly over both sides of the steaks.

5 Meanwhile, brush the tomato halves and onion slices with 2 tbsp of the olive oil.

6 Cook the steaks over high direct heat for 10–15 minutes (10 minutes for rare), turning once halfway through the cooking time. At the same time, cook the onion slices alongside the steaks for about 8 minutes and the tomato halves for 6 minutes, turning once halfway through the cooking time, until tender and charred. Remove the meat from the grill and let rest for 5 minutes.

Serves 4

7 Roughly chop the tomatoes and onions, and mix with the remaining olive oil, garlic, sherry vinegar, and chopped parsley or cilantro (coriander). Season to taste.

8 Serve the steaks with the warm tomato salsa.

Fillet of beef with black pepper and mustard crust

The mustard and pepper mixture forms a crust on the meat, which seals in the juices beautifully.

3 tbsp black peppercorns, coarsely crushed
4 tbsp Dijon mustard
1 tsp salt
2lb/ 900g fillet of beef

1 Preheat barbecue grill to medium indirect heat.

2 In a small bowl, mix together the black pepper and mustard to form a thick paste. Spread this evenly over the beef to completely coat it.

3 Cook the beef over medium indirect heat for 1–1 hour, 15 minutes (1 hour for rare).

4 Remove from the heat and let stand for 10 minutes before slicing thinly. Serve immediately.

Serves 4–6

Steak sandwich

Flank steak is an inexpensive and very flavorful cut of beef. Here, it is marinated to ensure that it is tender when barbecued rare or medium.

2 lb/1kg flank steak
salt and freshly ground black pepper

marinade
3 garlic cloves, crushed
1 tbsp chili sauce
1 tbsp Worcestershire sauce
3 tbsp olive oil
juice of 3 limes
1/2 cup/125ml tomato juice

mustard mayonnaise
1/2 quantity Homemade Mayonnaise
  (page 141)
1 tbsp grainy Dijon mustard
1 tbsp chopped fresh parsley

grilled mushrooms
2 tbsp olive oil
8 large flat mushrooms, such as field or
  portabella
2 ciabatta loaves, split horizontally, then cut
  in half crosswise

1 In a large re-sealable plastic bag, mix together the garlic, chili sauce, Worcestershire sauce, olive oil, lime juice, and tomato juice, and season with black pepper. Put the bag into a large shallow dish and add the steak, turning it to coat in the marinade. Marinate for at least 4 hours and preferably overnight, turning the steak occasionally in the marinade.

2 For the mustard mayonnaise, in a medium mixing bowl, mix together the mayonnaise, mustard, and parsley. Season, cover, and refrigerate until needed.

3 When ready to cook, preheat the barbecue grill to high direct heat.

4 Remove the meat from the marinade, reserving the marinade. Cook over high direct heat for 10–15 minutes for rare, and 15–18 minutes for medium, brushing once or twice with the marinade and turning once halfway through the cooking time.

5 Meanwhile, brush the mushrooms with the olive oil and season. Cook, gill-side-up, alongside the steak for about 8 minutes until tender. Do not turn the mushrooms or all the juices that gather in the gills will be lost.

6 Remove the meat and mushrooms from the barbecue and let stand for 10 minutes before slicing the steak across the grain.

7 Meanwhile, toast the ciabatta. Spread the 4 bottom pieces with the mustard mayonnaise. Divide the steak between the bread and add a mushroom to each. Top with the remaining bread and serve immediately.

Serves 4

HIGH ON THE HOG!

Planning to grill up some pork on your barbecue? Depending on the cut you choose, it responds really well to both slow cooking and fast grilling. Marinated or served with a sauce, it has a melting, luscious texture and a deliciously sweet flavor.

Always buy the best quality pork you can find. Pigs do not respond well to intensive rearing, and meat produced in this way is too lean and lacking in tenderness and flavor. Look for outdoor reared pork and if possible, choose organic products. You will be rewarded with succulent meat that is full of good, old-fashioned flavor.

Look for pork with a deep color—pale pink flesh often indicates a tasteless chop. The meat will usually have a good layer of fat and will sometimes have the rind attached. This can be easily removed, if you prefer. Joints of pork should also have a good layer of fat and/or rind. If

you're retaining the rind, score it with a small sharp knife or get your butcher to do this for you. This will help to produce a yummy crispy finish. When you get your joint or chops home, take them out of their wrapping and pat them dry with kitchen paper. It's important to remember that pork from supermarkets is often a little damp—and you'll never get a golden color from a wet piece of meat. If possible, leave it uncovered in the refrigerator until ready to cook—but no more than a day. This ensures that it's as dry as possible for grilling Because pork has such a mild flavor, it marries well with a wonderful variety of seasonings, including sage, rosemary, thyme, lemon, garlic, apple, and other sharp tasting flavors such as pineapple, cumin, chilies—the list goes on.

Almost all cuts of pork are suitable for the barbecue, with the exception of bacon, perhaps—though bacon is often used to wrap around other foods, such as shrimp. As with all meat, pork is best cooked on the bone. This helps to retain all its tenderness and succulence and also adds depth of flavor.

Ribs are the perfect choice for grilling as the meat is delicious-tasting, and slow cooking over an indirect heat helps to bring this out. Chops are excellent very simply grilled and then served with any of the barbecue sauces that you will find here. The classic Boston Butt (bone-in pork shoulder) is unbelievably tender when cooked slowly in a hot-sweet-sour barbecue sauce. Allow it to cool, then slice it and serve it on crusty rolls.

Whatever cut you choose, cook the meat carefully and you will be rewarded with a wonderfully tasty result. Enjoy!

Pork ribs in honey-orange chili adobo

These ribs are marinated overnight in a flavorful marinade before being cooked slowly until the meat almost falls off the bone. Don't be tempted to use baby back ribs for this recipe—try ordinary meaty ribs for a really succulent result.

Serves 4

2 tbsp chili seasoning
½ cup/125ml fresh orange juice
¼ cup/60ml olive oil
juice of 2 limes
3 garlic cloves, crushed
1 tbsp ground cumin
1 tbsp finely grated orange peel
2 tbsp honey
1 tbsp tomato paste (purée)
2 tsp dried oregano
6lb/2.7kg pork spareribs
salt and freshly ground black pepper

1 In a medium bowl, mix together everything, except the spareribs, and season with salt and pepper.

2 Put the ribs into a large re-sealable bag. Add the marinade and knead the bag, turning it until the ribs are well coated. Refrigerate for 24–48 hours, turning once or twice in the marinade.

3 Preheat barbecue grill to medium indirect heat.

4 Lift the ribs from the marinade, but don't brush off the excess.

5 Cook over medium indirect heat for 1–1 hour, 15 minutes, until tender, turning once halfway through the cooking time. If the sauce becomes too brown, cover with a little foil.

6 Remove from the heat and rest for 10 minutes. Separate the ribs and serve immediately.

Kansas City pork ribs

Kansas City barbecue sauce is slightly sweeter than Texas barbecue sauce, but you could reasonably substitute one for the other in this recipe if you happened to have some leftover. If you can't get baby back pork ribs, ordinary meaty ribs will do just as well.

1/2 cup/80g firmly packed
  dark brown sugar
1/2 onion, finely chopped
1 1/2 tsp celery seeds
1 1/2 tsp garlic powder
1 1/2 tsp chili seasoning
1 tsp finely ground black pepper
1 tsp ground cumin
1/2 tsp cayenne
2 cups/500ml tomato ketchup
1/4 cup/60ml white vinegar or more to taste
2 tbsp prepared yellow mustard
juice of 1 lime
1 tsp liquid smoke (optional)
4 tbsp butter, cubed and chilled
6lb/2.7kg baby back pork spareribs
salt and freshly ground black pepper

Serves 4

1 In a medium saucepan, combine all the ingredients, except the butter and spareribs. Bring to a boil, stirring to dissolve the sugar. You may want to have a lid handy to protect yourself and your kitchen from any sputtering. Reduce the heat and simmer for 25 minutes, stirring occasionally. With a whisk, blend in the butter cubes, a couple at a time, until incorporated. Set aside until needed.

3 Cook the ribs over medium indirect heat for 1–1 hour, 15 minutes, turning once halfway through cooking time, until very tender. Brush generously with the sauce during the last 10 minutes of cooking time.

4 Remove from the barbecue and let rest for 10 minutes. Carve into individual ribs and serve immediately with extra sauce.

Pork skewers with chilies and pineapple

This is a classic marriage of pork and pineapple. Serve the skewers with plain boiled rice.

Serves 4

2 pork tenderloins, about 1¾lb/800g
  total weight
½ fresh pineapple, cored and peeled
2 tsp black peppercorns
2 tsp paprika
1 tsp salt

ancho sauce
2 dried ancho chilies
1 cup/250ml boiling water
1 tbsp olive oil
1 small onion, finely chopped
1 garlic clove, crushed
½ cup/125ml ketchup
2 tbsp Worcestershire sauce
2 tbsp brown sugar
1 tbsp Dijon mustard
½ cup/125ml chicken stock
salt and freshly ground black pepper

Slow-cooked pork ribs with honey-mustard-vinegar mop

These ribs are for those who prefer their sauces with a little bite.

2 tbsp runny honey
2 tbsp prepared mustard or Dijon mustard
2 tsp coarsely cracked black peppercorns
1 cup/250ml cider vinegar
6lb/2.7kg pork spareribs
salt

1 To make the ancho sauce, put the chilies into a small bowl and cover with the boiling water. Let soak for 20 minutes until softened and swelled. Drain and remove the stems and seeds. Chop the flesh finely and set aside.

2 Heat the oil in a medium saucepan and add the onion. Cook for 5–7 minutes, until softened, then add the garlic and cook for another 1 minute. Add the remaining sauce ingredients and season to taste. Bring to a boil and simmer very gently, uncovered, for 1 hour, stirring often, until the onion is tender and the sauce has thickened.

3 Meanwhile, trim any excess fat and sinew from the pork and cut into 16 even-size chunks. Cut the pineapple into 16 similar-size chunks. Alternate pork and pineapple chunks on each of 4 metal or wooden skewers, spacing them slightly apart. Set aside.

4 Coarsely crush the black peppercorns, then mix with the paprika and salt. Sprinkle evenly over the skewers.

5 Meanwhile, preheat the barbecue grill to high direct heat.

6 Cook the skewers over high direct heat for about 4 minutes. Turn, brush generously with some of the sauce and cook for a further 3–4 minutes. Continue turning and brushing every 3–4 minutes, until the pork is crisp and browned and cooked through—about 15 minutes.

7 Serve immediately with extra sauce.

Serves 4

1 In a small bowl or jug, mix together the honey, mustard, black pepper, and cider vinegar. Set aside.

2 Preheat barbecue grill to medium indirect heat.

3 Cook the ribs over medium indirect heat for 1–1 hour, 15 minutes, mopping often with the vinegar mixture and turning once halfway through the cooking time, until tender and golden.

4 Remove from the heat and let stand for 10 minutes. Carve into individual ribs, season with salt to taste, and serve immediately.

Pork chops with bourbon-mustard sauce

Brining pork chops overnight actually changes the meat's cell structure, making it more tender and intensifying its flavor. The bourbon and mustard sauce makes a delicious accompaniment.

2/3 cup/200g kosher salt or sea salt
1/2 cup/80g packed brown sugar
4 bone-in pork loin chops
salt and freshly ground black pepper

bourbon-mustard sauce
1 1/2 tbsp unsalted butter
2 small shallots, finely chopped
1 garlic clove, crushed
1 hot red chili, seeded and finely chopped
1/2 cup/125ml good quality bourbon
3/4 cup/185ml whipping cream
3/4 cup/185ml beef stock
3 tbsp grainy Dijon mustard
1 tbsp chopped fresh parsley

1 To make the brine, bring about 8 cups/2lt of water to a boil in a large saucepan. Add the salt and sugar and stir until just dissolved. Remove from the heat and let cool to room temperature. In a shallow non-metallic container put the pork

Pork chops with tomato-habanero mop

A mop can be made with anything you have to hand that will add flavor to whatever you are cooking—some wine vinegar or even beer. This one is a bit more complicated, but adds plenty of flavor to the meat. If you are sensitive to chilies, wear rubber gloves when handling the habanero (Scotch bonnet), as they are particularly fiery.

2 fresh habanero (Scotch bonnet) chilies, seeded and finely chopped
1/2 cup/125ml tomato juice
1/2 small onion, grated
3 tbsp fresh orange juice
3 tbsp chopped fresh cilantro (coriander)
1 tbsp lime juice

Serves 4

1 garlic clove, crushed
4 pork chops, about 8oz/225g each
salt and freshly ground black pepper

chops in a single layer and pour the brine over. Cover and refrigerate for about 12 hours, turning the chops once or twice.

2 Drain the pork chops and discard the brine. Cover the chops with fresh cold water and let stand for 1 hour. Drain and repeat. Drain again and pat dry with paper towel.

3 Preheat the barbecue grill to medium direct heat.

4 Season the chops with black pepper and cook over medium direct heat for 12–15 minutes, until golden and cooked through. Remove from the heat and let stand for 5 minutes.

5 Meanwhile to make the sauce, melt the butter in a small heavy saucepan over a low heat. Add the shallots, garlic,

and chili and cook gently for 5–7 minutes, until softened but not browned. Add the bourbon and increase the heat to high. Simmer rapidly for 2–3 minutes, until reduced by half.

6 Whisk the cream, beef stock, and mustard into the sauce. Bring to a boil and simmer, uncovered, stirring occasionally, until the sauce is reduced by about one third and has thickened slightly. Add the parsley, season to taste, and keep warm.

7 Put the cooked chops onto individual serving plates and spoon over the sauce. Serve immediately.

Serves 4

1 Preheat the barbecue grill to medium direct heat.

2 In the bowl of a food processor or blender, put the chilies, tomato juice, onion, orange juice, cilantro (coriander), lime juice, and garlic, then blend until puréed. Transfer to a jug or bowl and set aside.

3 Season the pork chops and cook over medium direct heat for 12–15 minutes, turning once halfway through the cooking time, until golden and cooked through. Mop often with the sauce,

allowing some to fall through the grill and onto the coals (the steam adds flavor too).

4 Remove the chops from the grill and let stand for 5 minutes before serving.

Pork steaks in chili-orange rub

Try to get nice thick-cut boneless pork steaks for this dish—thinner steaks have a tendency to become dry. Serve with Spiced Grilled Sweet Potatoes (page 130), and Coleslaw with Jalapeño and Mango (page 138).

1 tbsp coriander seeds
1 tsp cumin seeds
1 tsp dried oregano
1 tsp hot dried chili flakes
finely grated peel of 1 orange
4 pork steaks, about 8oz/225g each
salt and freshly ground black pepper

1 Preheat the barbecue grill to medium direct heat.

2 Heat a small dry frying pan and add the coriander and cumin seeds. Cook over a high heat for 1–2 minutes, until the seeds darken and become aromatic. Transfer to a mortar and pestle or spice grinder and let cool. Add the oregano and chili flakes and grind to a fine powder.

Stir in the orange peel and season to taste.

3 Wash the pork steaks and pat dry with paper towel. Sprinkle evenly with the spice mixture and rub in well.

4 Cook the steaks over medium direct heat for 12–15 minutes, turning once halfway through the cooking time, until golden and cooked through.

5 Remove from the grill and let stand for 5 minutes before serving.

Serves 4

Grilled pork shoulder with chipotle-orange mop

This is another recipe which requires very long, slow cooking. You may prefer to finish this dish in the oven, once the initial smoking time is finished. Otherwise, be prepared to be on hand to keep the fire going.

2 cups/500ml fresh orange juice
4 tbsp chipotles in adobo
6 tbsp packed brown sugar
juice of 2 limes
6lb/2.7kg bone-in pork shoulder
salt and freshly ground black pepper

You will also need smoking chips or chunks (of your choice), which have been soaked appropriately and drained before cooking.

Serves 6

1 Preheat barbecue grill to medium indirect heat.

2 In a small bowl or jug, mix together the orange juice, chipotles, brown sugar, and lime juice.

3 Season the pork shoulder with salt and pepper. Add the smoking chips or chunks to the barbecue. Reduce the heat to low, if using a gas barbecue, or see page 8 for adjusting charcoal barbecues. Cook the pork shoulder for 3–4 hours, mopping the meat every 30 minutes and turning it occasionally. Try to maintain a temperature of about 250–275°F/120–140°C, gas ½–1. The exact timing is not important because the meat will continue to tenderize, even after 6 hours as long as the temperature is low.

4 Serve hot, warm or cold.

Pulled pork shoulder

This kind of pulled pork is often served with a vinegar-based sauce. Here, however, it is tossed with a creamy mustard dressing and served on French bread or crusty rolls with shredded cabbage for a crunchy contrast.

4½lb/2kg boneless
  pork shoulder
8 crusty rolls or 1 loaf
  French bread, to serve
2 cups/200g shredded red
  cabbage, to serve

the rub

2 tbsp paprika
1 tbsp light soft brown sugar
1 tbsp chili seasoning
1 tbsp ground cumin
1½ tsp coarsely ground black pepper
2 tsp salt

creamy mustard dressing

½ quantity Homemade Mayonnaise
  (page 141)
2 tbsp crème fraîche
1 heaped tbsp grainy Dijon mustard
  1–2 tsp Tabasco, to taste

Serves 4

1 Mix together the paprika, sugar, chili seasoning, cumin, black pepper, and salt. Open up the pork shoulder and rub thoroughly with the spice mixture, inside and out. Let marinate for 1 hour, or more if you have time.

2 Preheat barbecue grill to medium indirect heat.

3 Cook the pork for 2½–3 hours, turning occasionally, until golden and very tender.

4 Remove the pork from the barbecue and let stand for 20 minutes.

5 Meanwhile, in a large bowl, mix together the mayonnaise, crème fraîche, and mustard, and season to taste. Set aside.

6 Using two forks, pull the meat into chunks or large shreds. Add the meat to the bowl with the mayonnaise mixture and toss everything together well.

7 Split the rolls in two horizontally. If using French bread, cut into 4 inch/10cm long pieces, then split these horizontally. Fill with the pork mixture and top with shredded cabbage. Serve immediately.

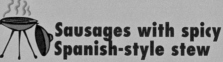

Sausages with spicy Spanish-style stew

You will need to find small, uncooked chorizo sausages for this gutsy dish. Another alternative is pastourma, a strongly flavored Greek sausage.

1½lb/675g new potatoes, halved
3 tbsp olive oil
1 red onion, chopped
1 tsp dried chili flakes
2 tsp smoked paprika
4 garlic cloves, crushed
1lb/450g fresh ripe tomatoes, skinned and chopped
14oz/400g can chickpeas, drained and rinsed
2 bay leaves
1lb/450g uncooked chorizo sausages
4 tbsp chopped fresh parsley, to garnish

Serves 4

Sausages with chili sauce and pot beans

Pork sausages are excellent for barbecuing as they are full of flavor and cook quickly. Here, they are livened up with a homemade chili sauce and served with Pot Beans. Buy sausages with a meat content of at least 90 per cent—organic brands are often a good bet.

2 tbsp Chili Paste (page 39)
2 tsp wine vinegar
1 garlic clove, crushed
1 tsp sugar
2lb/1kg good quality pork sausages (see introduction)
2 cups/450ml Pot Beans (page 126)
salt and freshly ground black pepper

1 Cook the potatoes in boiling salted water for 12–15 minutes, until tender. Drain well and set aside.

2 Heat the oil in a large, deep frying pan or wok. Add the onion and cook over a medium heat for 5–7 minutes, until softened and starting to color. Add the chili flakes, paprika, and garlic and cook for a further 30 seconds. Add the tomatoes, potatoes, chickpeas, bay leaves, and 2/3 cup/150ml water. Bring to a boil and simmer for 10 minutes, until thickened and piping hot.

3 Meanwhile, preheat barbecue grill to high direct heat.

4 Cook the chorizo sausages over high direct heat for 10–12 minutes, turning often, until tender and golden.

5 Remove from the heat and let stand for 5 minutes. Chop roughly and serve with the chickpea stew. Garnish with chopped parsley.

Serves 4

1 Preheat the barbecue grill to high direct heat.

2 In a small bowl, mix together the chili paste, wine vinegar, garlic, and sugar. Season to taste and set aside.

3 Cook the sausages over high direct heat for 8–10 minutes, turning often, until golden and just cooked through.

4 Serve immediately, with the chili sauce and a spoonful of beans.

LAMB FOR FINE FLAVOR

Lamb is becoming an increasingly popular red meat. It has a meltingly sweet flavor and it grills beautifully. Look out for 'new season' lamb which will have the best flavor of all.

Almost any cut of lamb can be successfully barbecued. Most cuts will benefit from being served at least a little pink. This is, of course, a matter of personal preference—the main objective being not to overcook it and end up with tough meat.

Look for lamb that has a good deep red color. It will usually have a good margin of fat and although the excess should always be removed before grilling, a little fat is necessary to ensure good flavor and moistness. When buying chops, make sure they've been butchered carefully—it's difficult to judge your timings if one chop is much thicker than the others.

Flavorings that are just fabulous with lamb are garlic, rosemary, thyme, lemon, cumin and chilli. For a quick marinade for chops, mix together a handful of lightly pounded thyme and rosemary leaves, a crushed garlic clove, the juice and peel of a lemon and a couple of tablespoons of olive oil. Pour this over some lamb chops and leave for about 20–30 minutes. Grill over a direct heat for 6–8 minutes until medium-rare. Delicious!

Lamb is a fatty meat, though, and it can flare up if you are not careful. This may spoil the meat by burning it. Avoid too much oil in any marinade and remove any excess fat from larger cuts, such as legs. Be vigilant whilst cooking and have ready a spray bottle of water to deal with severe problems.

Leg of lamb can be cooked on the bone if you cook it indirectly. Keep the temperature on the medium to low side to avoid overcooking it.

A rack of lamb has all the chops still attached to each other. Get your butcher to French trim the bones for you—which means that he (or she) will remove all the excess fat and flesh from between them. The chine bone should also be removed so that the rack can be carved easily when cooked. Racks of lamb come with a fatty piece across the meat. This must be removed for grilling or it will catch fire. It peels away easily along with a small

amount of meat, but you don't need it for flavor or tenderness as a rack of lamb has plenty of both.

Lamb is a classic Middle Eastern ingredient for kabobs (kebabs). In addition to the Moroccan-style recipe here, try threading some chunks of lamb onto skewers then marinating in a mixture of lemon juice, ground cumin, garlic and fresh cilantro. Grill for 8–10 minutes then serve in pitta bread with hummous and salad.

Spiced butterflied leg of lamb

Boning a leg of lamb is a skilled job, so it's probably easier to get your butcher to do it for you. The advantage for the barbecue-cook is that without the bone, the meat lays flat and cooks very quickly, thereby remaining tender, but also providing bits ranging from rare to well-done—something for everyone. Lamb does have a tendency to flare up on the barbecue, however, so some vigilance is required during cooking.

1 tbsp cumin seeds
1 tbsp coriander seeds
1 tsp black peppercorns
2 tsp hot dried chili flakes
½ tsp cinnamon
2 tsp salt, or to taste
5lb/2.25kg leg of lamb, butterflied

1 Preheat the barbecue grill to medium direct heat.

2 Heat a small dry frying pan and when hot, add the cumin seeds, coriander seeds, and black peppercorns. Cook for 1–2 minutes, until the seeds darken and become aromatic. Remove from the heat and transfer to a spice grinder or mortar and pestle. Let cool. Add the dried chili flakes and grind to a coarse powder. Stir in the cinnamon and about 2 tsp salt.

Serves 8

3 Lay the lamb flat on a chopping board or clean work surface. Sprinkle with about half the spice mixture and rub in well. Turn the meat and sprinkle with the remaining spice mixture, again rubbing in well.

4 Cook over medium direct heat for 20–30 minutes, turning once halfway through the cooking time. Watch carefully for flareups, particularly when cooking skin-side-down.

5 Remove from the heat and let rest for 10 minutes before slicing thickly. Serve immediately.

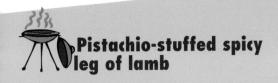

Pistachio-stuffed spicy leg of lamb

It is worth getting your butcher to bone the lamb for you so that you end up with a neat parcel when the meat is stuffed and re-formed.

Serves 6–8

3 tbsp olive oil
2 garlic cloves, finely chopped
1 cup/125g shelled pistachios, roughly chopped
1 hot green chili, seeded and finely chopped
finely grated peel of 2 oranges
4 tbsp chopped fresh mint
2 tbsp chopped fresh parsley
5lb/2.25kg boneless leg of lamb
4–5 large sprigs fresh rosemary
salt and freshly ground black pepper

1 Preheat barbecue grill to medium indirect heat.

2 Heat the olive oil in a small frying pan. Add the garlic, pistachios, and chili and cook over a medium heat for 2–3 minutes, until the garlic and chili are softened and the pistachios are lightly toasted.

3 Remove from the heat and transfer to a medium bowl. Add the orange peel, mint, and parsley. Season to taste and mix together well.

4 Lay the meat flat on a chopping board or clean work surface, skin-side-down. Spread the herb and pistachio mixture evenly over the meat, pressing it in well. Re-roll the meat to form a neat parcel, then tie with string. Season the meat with salt and pepper.

5 Cook over medium indirect heat for 1 hour, 15–30 minutes, turning often, until medium-rare. The shorter cooking time is for rare meat.

6 Remove from the barbecue and let rest for 10 minutes before carving. Serve immediately.

Pecan-crusted rack of lamb

Rack of lamb always looks impressive, and cooks very quickly too. It's important to remove the thick layer of fat from the meat side of the racks to avoid excessive flare-ups.

2 tbsp harissa or homemade Chili Paste
   (page 39)
2 tbsp chopped fresh parsley
1 garlic clove, crushed
1 tbsp grainy Dijon mustard
2 racks of lamb, 6 ribs each
1 cup/100g pecans, finely chopped
salt and freshly ground black pepper

1 Preheat the barbecue grill to medium direct heat.

Serves 4

2 In a small bowl, mix together the harissa or chili paste, parsley, garlic, and mustard. Set aside.

3 Remove the layer of fat from the back of the racks of lamb. You will have to remove a little of the meat as well, but the lamb will cook more quickly with less flareups. Season to taste.

4 Cook the racks of lamb, bone-side-down, for 10 minutes over medium direct heat. Remove the meat from the barbecue and spread the harissa mixture over the cooked side. Press the pecans into the harissa-coated meat until well covered.

5 Return the lamb to the barbecue, pecan-side-up, and cook for a further 15 minutes. The lamb will be medium-rare. Add another 5–10 minutes if you prefer the meat more well-done, but do not overcook. You may also need to cover the pecan nuts with foil to prevent them from burning.

6 Remove from the heat and let rest for 10 minutes. Carve into individual cutlets or into groups of 3 ribs and serve immediately.

Lamb and eggplant kabobs

These skewers have a real Moroccan flavor.

1 large eggplant (aubergine)
1 tsp cumin seeds
2 tsp coriander seeds
2 tsp finely grated fresh ginger
2 garlic cloves, crushed
1 small hot red chili, seeded and
  finely chopped
2lb/1kg lamb neck fillet
salt and freshly ground black pepper

chickpea salad
1 garlic clove, crushed
juice of 1 lemon
1 tbsp tahini (sesame seed paste)
3 tbsp extra virgin olive oil
2 tbsp chopped fresh mint
2 tbsp chopped fresh cilantro (coriander)
1 tbsp chopped fresh parsley
12 cherry tomatoes, halved
1 small red onion, finely chopped
14oz/400g can chickpeas, rinsed

1 Preheat the barbecue grill to high direct heat.

Serves 4

2 Put the cumin seeds and coriander seeds into a spice grinder or mortar and pestle and grind to a fine powder. Stir in the ginger, garlic, and red chili. Season to taste and set aside.

3 Cut the neck fillet into 16 large chunks. Put the meat into a medium bowl and add the ginger mixture. Knead until the meat is well coated.

4 Slice the eggplant (aubergine) crosswise into rounds, about 1 inch/2.5cm thick, then cut these into half-moon shapes. Thread the pieces of neck fillet and eggplant (aubergine) alternately onto 4 large skewers. Brush with the olive oil.

5 Cook the lamb and eggplant (aubergine) skewers over high direct heat for 8–10 minutes, turning often, until golden and tender.

6 Meanwhile, in a medium bowl, whisk together the garlic, lemon juice, tahini, olive oil, and chopped herbs. Stir in the tomatoes, onion, and chickpeas, and season to taste.

7 Remove the skewers from the barbecue and serve immediately with the chickpea salad.

SIZZLING FISH AND SHELLFISH

Nothing tastes better in the open air than fresh fish and shellfish broiled to perfection on the barbecue. This is great news, because fish and seafood are becoming increasingly popular as more people realize just how healthy, easily prepared and tasty these foods are. A freshly caught fish has always been the natural choice for enthusiastic anglers to cook over a campfire—whether it's on the beach or at the riverside. "Straight out of the water and onto the grill" has always been the motto for these folk.

But even if you're not able to get out there into the wild and haul in your own catch, nowadays you should have no problem obtaining whatever fish or seafood your heart desires. Modern methods of storage and transportation deliver a dazzling array of choice from all over the world to your local fishmonger and nearest large supermarket. There, displayed on the fresh fish shelves, you'll be amazed at the sheer variety that is on offer.

There are several key guidelines to keep in mind when you're shopping for fish—the first being to ensure that you buy from a reliable supplier, preferably on the same day that you're going to cook it. A well-informed fishmonger is a great asset if you want to be sure of getting the best—so it's important to build up a good relationship. Specialists always like to pass on their knowledge, so ask questions, and show a genuine interest. For instance, an experienced fishmonger will be glad to advise you about unfamiliar fish, and suggest what types would be suitable for grilling on the barbecue.

Freshness is your key consideration when buying fish. So how can you tell? The two main giveaways are appearance and odor. Look at the fish closely: the scales should be bright, shiny and tightly arranged; the eyes should look bright, not cloudy; and the gills must bright red rather than dull pink. As for the odor, fresh fish has a delicate, sweetish smell, as opposed to 'fishy'. If you're looking at fillets, check that the flesh is translucent, not opaque, and that it is firm and clear, with no dark spots. If you get a chance to feel the fish, press the surface to check that the flesh is firm and resistant.

Once you've tried out some of these fabulous fish dishes on your barbecue, you'll be able to appreciate the sheer versatility of what's on offer here: for instance, you can choose a sizzling Red-hot Salmon with fiery Oriental spices, Tuna Steaks with Roasted Red Bell Pepper and Chili Butter Sauce, Spiced Catfish with Avocado Sauce (you could use trout instead—it tastes just as good), and Bream with Garlic and Cilantro Butter. These are just a few examples to give you instant inspiration, and set you on the road to a great new style of cooking hot'n spicy fish and seafood.

Soft shell crabs with chipotle, lime, and cilantro mayo

Soft-shell crabs are a seasonal delicacy, available fresh in springtime when young crabs shed their hard shells. They are available frozen at other times of the year. They are generally served fried but here are simply marinated and barbecued, then served with a delicious spicy mayonnaise.

finely grated peel and juice of 2 limes
1/3 cup/60ml olive oil
2 garlic cloves, crushed
1/2 tsp cayenne
12 small soft-shell crabs, cleaned (the crabs should be about 2–2 1/2 inches/5–6cm)
1 quantity Homemade Mayonnaise (page 141), made with lime juice in place of lemon juice or vinegar
1 tbsp chipotles in adobo
3 tbsp chopped fresh cilantro (coriander)
salt and freshly ground black pepper

1 In a large, shallow, non-metallic dish, mix together the lime juice and peel, olive oil, garlic, and cayenne. Season lightly and add the crabs in a single layer, if possible (if necessary, use 2 dishes). Turn the crabs to coat well in the mixture and set aside for 30 minutes.

2 Preheat the barbecue grill to medium direct heat.

3 Cook the crabs over direct medium heat for 5–8 minutes, until golden and cooked through.

4 Meanwhile, put the mayonnaise into a small bowl and add the chipotles in adobo and the cilantro (coriander). Season to taste and set aside until needed.

5 Divide the crabs between serving plates and pass round the mayonnaise for everyone to help themselves.

Serves 4

Giant shrimp wrapped in bacon with Mexican barbecue sauce

These shrimp (prawns) make a great appetizer, or can be served as part of a larger barbecue menu.

1lb/450g raw whole shrimp (prawns), about 16–20, shell-on
8 slices prosciutto or smoked bacon
2 tbsp olive oil
juice of 1 lemon
1 cup/250ml Mexican Adobo Barbecue Sauce (page 40)
salt and freshly ground black pepper
lemon wedges, to serve

Serves 4

1 Preheat the barbecue grill to high direct heat.

2 Remove the heads and shells from the shrimp (prawns) but leave the tails intact. Remove the black vein that runs down the back of the shrimp (prawn) and discard. Wash and dry the shrimp (prawns) on paper towel.

3 Slice the prosciutto in half lengthwise. If using bacon, use the back of a knife to stretch it. Wrap each shrimp (prawn) in a piece of prosciutto or bacon.

4 Mix together the olive oil and lemon juice. Brush the mixture over the shrimp (prawns). Cook over high direct heat for 6–7 minutes, turning once, until the prosciutto or bacon is browned and crisp and the shrimp (prawns) have turned pink. Brush with the barbecue sauce during the last 2–3 minutes of cooking.

5 Serve the shrimp (prawns) immediately with lemon wedges.

Sweet red chili salmon steaks with black bean and corn salsa

The sweet red chili and honey marinade flavors the salmon, but also gives it a beautiful glazed finish. The real star here, however, is the smoky corn and bean salsa. Simply sensational!

1 tbsp runny honey
2 small hot red chilies,
   seeded and finely chopped
juice of 1 lime
1 tbsp olive oil
4 salmon steaks, about
   8oz/225g each

Serves 4

black bean and corn salsa

3 garlic cloves, peeled
2 jalapeño chilies
2 tbsp olive oil
3 long green chilies, such as Anaheim
   or New Mexico
1 large corn cob, husks and silks removed
1 large tomato
juice of 2 limes
2 tbsp tequila
7oz/200g can black beans, drained and
   rinsed, or 3/4 cup/200g cooked dried
   black beans
1 small red onion, finely chopped
3 tbsp chopped fresh cilantro (coriander)
salt and freshly ground black pepper

1 Preheat the barbecue grill to high direct heat.

2 Mix together the honey, chilies, lime juice, and olive oil. Put the salmon steaks into a shallow non-metallic dish and pour the marinade over. Cover and let marinate for 30 minutes.

3 Meanwhile to make the salsa, put the garlic cloves and jalapeños onto a small skewer. Brush the garlic, jalapeños, long green chilies, and corn with the olive oil. Transfer the vegetables to the barbecue and cook for about 8–12 minutes, until everything is softened and charred, removing them from the barbecue when cooked. Transfer the chilies to a plastic bag and leave until cool enough to handle.

4 Roughly chop the garlic. Peel the chilies and remove the stems and seeds. Roughly chop the flesh. Seed and roughly chop the tomatoes. Remove the kernels from the corn cobs.

5 In a blender or food processor, combine the tomato, jalapeños, garlic, lime juice, and tequila. Process until fairly smooth.

6 In a medium mixing bowl, add the puréed mixture along with the remaining chopped chilies, corn kernels, black beans, red onion, and cilantro (coriander). Season to taste. Cover and let stand at room temperature until needed.

7 Lift the salmon steaks from the marinade, brushing off any excess. Transfer to the barbecue and cook over high direct heat for 6–8 minutes, turning once and brushing occasionally with the marinade, until browned and just cooked through.

8 Remove the salmon steaks from the barbecue and serve immediately with the salsa.

Tuna steaks with roasted red bell pepper and chili butter sauce

Tuna is a meaty fish, with a very firm flesh. Be careful not to overcook the fish, since it is at its best when still pink in the center.

1/2 tsp black peppercorns
juice of 1 lemon
4 tuna steaks, about 7–8oz/200–225g each

roasted red pepper and chili sauce

2 red bell peppers
1 tbsp olive oil
1 tbsp harissa or homemade Chili Paste
  (see Chili-rubbed Cornish Hens, page 39)
1/2 cup/120g unsalted butter
juice of 1 lemon
salt and freshly ground black pepper

1 Heat a small dry frying pan, add the black peppercorns and fry over a high heat for 1–2 minutes until they become aromatic. Remove from the heat and let cool. Grind finely in a mortar and pestle or using a spice grinder.

2 In a small bowl, mix together the ground black pepper and lemon juice. Set aside.

3 Preheat barbecue grill to high direct heat.

4 To make the sauce, brush the peppers with the olive oil and transfer to the barbecue. Cook for 7–8 minutes, turning often, until the skin has blackened. Transfer the peppers to a plastic bag and leave until cool enough to handle. Peel off the skin and remove the stems and seeds.

5 Put the peppers into a food processor, along with the harissa or chili paste, butter, and lemon juice. Process until smooth. Season to taste. Scrape into a bowl and set aside until needed.

6 Brush the tuna steaks with the lemon and black pepper mixture. Cook over high direct heat for 2–4 minutes, turning once during cooking until golden but not quite cooked through.

7 Serve immediately with the red pepper sauce.

Serves 4

Grilled grouper with black pepper and lemon mayonnaise

Grouper has a unique flavor and firm texture, which is perfectly complemented by the creamy mayonnaise. If, for some reason, you cannot find grouper, bream makes an excellent substitute.

Serves 4

4 grouper fillets, each about 6–7oz/ 175–200g

black pepper and lemon mayonnaise

1 egg yolk
1 tsp Dijon mustard
juice of 2 lemons and finely grated peel of 1
1 tsp coarsely cracked black peppercorns
3/4 cup/ 185ml olive oil
1/2 cup/ 125ml vegetable oil
1 tbsp chopped fresh parsley
salt

1 In a food processor, or in the jug of a stick blender, whisk together the egg yolk, mustard, juice and peel of 1 lemon, the black pepper, and salt until foamy.

2 With the motor running, gradually add the olive and vegetable oils in a very slow but steady stream until the mixture is thick and pale. If the mixture is too thick, add about 1 tbsp hot water until thinned to the desired consistency. Stir in the chopped parsley and set aside until needed.

3 Preheat the barbecue grill to high direct heat.

4 Season the grouper fillets. Drizzle with the remaining lemon juice. Cook the grouper fillets over high direct heat for 7–8 minutes, turning once, until golden and the fish just flakes.

5 Serve immediately with the black pepper and lemon mayonnaise.

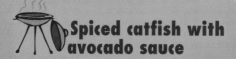

Spiced catfish with avocado sauce

Well flavored, with nice firm flesh, catfish is a popular favorite. If you wish you could use seabass in this recipe.

1 tsp cayenne
1 tsp ground cumin
½ tsp brown sugar
4 catfish fillets, each
  about 6–7oz/175–200g
1 large avocado
4 tbsp unsalted butter, softened
2 tbsp mayonnaise
1 garlic clove, crushed
2 tbsp chopped fresh chives
1 hot red chili, seeded and finely chopped
salt and freshly ground black pepper

Serves 4

1 Preheat the barbecue grill to high direct heat.

2 Mix together the cayenne, cumin, and brown sugar, and season to taste. Rub the mixture into the fish fillets and set aside for 30 minutes.

3 Halve the avocado and remove the stone. Peel, then chop the flesh roughly. Put the chopped avocado into a bowl along with the butter and mash together, leaving some lumps of avocado. Stir in the mayonnaise, garlic, chives, and chili, and season to taste. Set aside until needed.

4 Cook the catfish fillets over high direct heat for 7–8 minutes, turning once during cooking, until golden and the flesh just flakes.

5 Serve immediately with the avocado sauce.

Bream with garlic and cilantro butter

A whole fish makes a delicious change for a barbecue. As with meat, leaving the flesh on the bones keeps it moist and improves the flavor. Get your fishmonger to clean and scale the fish for you.

1 tbsp brown sugar
1 tsp freshly ground black pepper
1 tsp salt
4 small bream or 2 large bream, about
  4lb/ 1.75kg total weight
1/2 cup/ 120g unsalted butter, softened
2 garlic cloves, crushed
2 tbsp chopped fresh cilantro (coriander)
juice and finely grated peel of 1 lemon
1 tbsp hot chili flakes, such as jalapeño
salt and freshly ground black pepper
lemon wedges, to serve

1 Mix together the brown sugar, black pepper, and salt. Rub the mixture into the skin of the fish. Set aside.

2 In a medium mixing bowl, beat the butter with the garlic, cilantro (coriander), lemon peel, and chili flakes, and season to taste. When thoroughly mixed, add the lemon juice and beat until incorporated. Scrape the mixture onto a large piece of waxed paper and, using the paper to help you, shape into a log. Enclose the butter in the paper and twist the ends together to seal. Refrigerate until needed.

3 Preheat the barbecue grill to high direct heat.

4 Cook the fish over high direct heat for 8–12 minutes, turning once halfway through the cooking time, until the skin is crisp and golden and the flesh just flakes. Remove from the heat and transfer to serving plates (if using small bream) or cut into fillets (if using larger fish).

5 Slice the butter thickly and put 1–2 slices on top of the fish. Serve immediately with lemon wedges.

Chili shrimp with sweet and spicy dipping sauce

Simplicity itself to make, the chili sauce is a perfect foil for the shrimp (prawns).

2¼lb/ 1kg raw jumbo shrimp (prawns)
2 tbsp vegetable oil
2 hot red chilies, seeded and finely chopped
3 garlic cloves, finely chopped
finely grated peel of 1 lemon
¼ cup/ 55g granulated (caster) sugar
3 tbsp rice or white
   wine vinegar
½ tsp salt
1 tsp hot chili
   flakes

Serves 4

1 Preheat the barbecue grill to high direct heat.

2 Wash and dry the shrimp (prawns). In a shallow, non-metallic dish, mix together the vegetable oil, chilies, garlic and lemon peel. Add the shrimp (prawns) and mix well. Set aside for 30 minutes.

3 Meanwhile, in a small saucepan, mix together the sugar, vinegar, salt, and chili flakes. Stir over a low heat until the sugar dissolves, then increase the heat. Bring to a boil, then reduce the heat and simmer gently for 2 minutes. Remove from the heat and transfer to a small bowl to cool. When cold, divide between 4 small bowls and set aside.

4 Thread the shrimp (prawns) onto metal or wooden skewers (it doesn't matter how many, as they'll be removed for serving—the skewers make turning the prawns much easier). Cook the shrimp (prawns) for 6–7 minutes, until pink and just cooked through.

5 Remove from the heat and carefully remove the shrimp (prawns) from the skewers onto individual serving dishes. Serve each plate with a bowl of the dipping sauce.

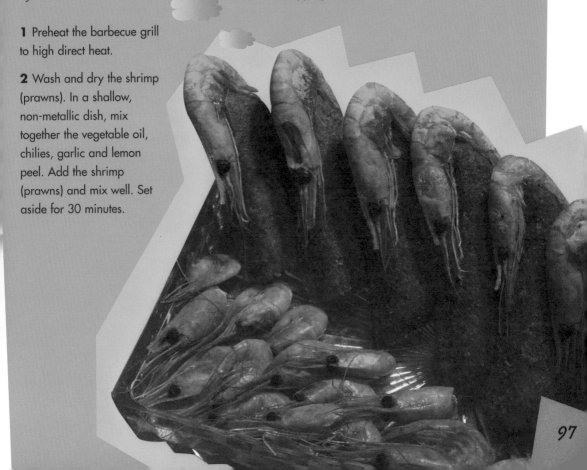

Whole red snapper with chili, herb and lemon rub

If you make the rub with dried herbs, it will keep for about 2 weeks in the refrigerator. If you use fresh herbs, use it immediately.

4 large garlic cloves, finely chopped
finely grated peel of 2 lemons
2 hot red chilies, seeded and finely chopped
1 tsp chopped fresh rosemary, or
½ tsp dried rosemary
1 tbsp chopped fresh basil,
or 1 tsp dried basil

Serves 4

2 tsp chopped fresh thyme leaves
or ½ tsp dried thyme
1 tbsp brown sugar
2 whole red snapper, about
2½–3lb/ 1kg–1.5kg total weight, cleaned
and scaled
salt and freshly ground black pepper

1 Preheat the barbecue grill to medium direct heat.

2 Mix together the garlic, lemon peel, chilies, rosemary, basil, thyme, and sugar, and season generously with salt and pepper.

3 Cut 3 or 4 slashes in each side of the fish, down to the bone. Rub with the herb mixture, making sure to get it into the slashes.

4 Cook over medium direct heat for 10–12 minutes, until golden and cooked through. Serve immediately.

Red-hot salmon

This fiery salmon dish has a distinctly Oriental flavor. The cucumber salad that accompanies it can be made well in advance, leaving you to cook the fish at the last minute for an impressive meal.

4 salmon steaks or fillets, skin-on, about 8oz/225g each

marinade

1 garlic clove, crushed
1 lemongrass stem, finely chopped
2–3 red chilies, to taste, seeded and finely sliced
juice and finely grated peel of 1 lime
2 tbsp Thai fish sauce
4 tbsp sunflower oil

cucumber salad

2 tbsp peanut oil
2 tbsp sunflower oil
1 garlic clove, chopped
1 shallot, chopped
1 red chili, seeded and finely shredded
2 tbsp Thai fish sauce
juice of 1 lime
1 tsp brown sugar
½ English cucumber, seeded and finely sliced
4 green (spring) onions, finely chopped
2oz/50g bean sprouts
2oz/50g roasted peanuts, roughly chopped
2 tbsp chopped fresh cilantro (coriander)

Serves 4

1 Preheat the barbecue grill to direct medium heat.

2 To make the marinade, in a shallow, non-metallic dish, mix together the garlic, lemongrass, chilies, lime juice and peel, fish sauce, and sunflower oil. Add the salmon steaks, turning to coat. Cover and set aside for 1 hour.

3 Meanwhile, heat the peanut and sunflower oils in a small frying pan. Add the garlic, shallot, and chili, and cook over a high heat for 2–3 minutes, until just starting to colour. Carefully add the fish sauce, lime juice, and sugar, and continue cooking for another 30 seconds or so until the sugar has dissolved and the mixture is bubbling. Remove to a small bowl and let cool.

4 In a serving bowl, mix together the cucumber, green (spring) onions and bean sprouts. Pour over the cooled dressing and toss together well. Set aside until needed.

5 Remove the salmon steaks from the marinade, shaking off any excess. Cook over direct medium heat for 6–8 minutes, turning once, until golden and tender.

6 Add the peanuts and cilantro (coriander) to the salad and toss together. Serve with the salmon steaks.

Salmon fillets with red bell pepper salsa & margarita mayonnaise

This is a real showstopper. Serve as part of a buffet or for a very special dinner party.

1 whole salmon, about 6½lb/3kg, scaled and filleted

8 tbsp chopped fresh mixed herbs, such as basil, parsley, chives, and cilantro (coriander)

2 tbsp green peppercorns in brine, drained

finely grated peel of 1 lime

6 tbsp vermouth or dry white wine

Serves 10

salt and freshly ground black pepper
lime wedges and fresh herb sprigs, to
  garnish

roasted red bell pepper dressing
1 red bell pepper
2 tsp olive oil
½ cup/125ml white wine vinegar
1¼ cups/300ml light olive oil
2 tsp chili sauce
5 green (spring) onions
1 tbsp chopped fresh parsley
2 tbsp chopped fresh chives

margarita mayonnaise
1 quantity fresh Homemade
  Mayonnaise (page 141)
2 tbsp tequila
juice of 1 lime
2 tbsp capers, drained and
  roughly chopped
1 tbsp Dijon mustard
1 tbsp chopped fresh
  basil

1 For the salmon, wash and dry the fillets. Set aside. Mix together the herbs, green peppercorns, and lime peel. Spread the mixture over the flesh side of one fillet. Top with the second fillet, flesh-side-down, and wrap in a double thickness of aluminum foil. Refrigerate for 1 hour.

2 When ready to cook the salmon, preheat the barbecue grill to high direct heat.

3 To make the roasted red bell pepper dressing, brush the red bell pepper with the olive oil and cook over high direct heat for 6–8 minutes, turning often, until charred and blackened. Transfer to a plastic bag until cool enough to handle.

4 Meanwhile, reduce the temperature to medium indirect heat or move the coals to indirect position.

5 Open the foil parcel containing the salmon. Drizzle in the vermouth or white wine and re-seal the parcel. Cook indirectly over medium heat for 1¼ hours until cooked through. Remove from the heat and let rest for 10 minutes.

6 Meanwhile, for the dressing, peel the cooled pepper and remove the stem and seeds, then chop finely and set aside. In a small serving bowl, whisk together the white wine vinegar, light olive oil, and chili sauce. Stir in the chopped pepper, green (spring) onions, and herbs. Season to taste and set aside.

7 For the margarita mayonnaise, in a small serving bowl, mix together the mayonnaise, tequila, lime juice, capers, mustard, and basil. Season to taste and set aside.

8 To serve the salmon, slice thickly crosswise. Transfer to a large serving platter, along with the 2 sauces. Garnish with lime wedges and sprigs of fresh herbs.

Lobster with orange chili butter

For a romantic picnic meal, what could be better than this very special lobster dish? Serve with chilled Champagne.

1 live lobster, about 1½lb/675g
½ cup/120g unsalted butter
1 hot red chili, seeded and finely chopped
1 garlic clove, crushed
finely grated peel and juice of 1 orange
1 tbsp fresh thyme leaves
1 tbsp chopped fresh parsley
salt and freshly ground black pepper

1 To prepare the lobster, lay it on a chopping board with the head pointing towards you. Insert the tip of a large sharp knife where the tail meets the head and split the head in two. Repeat with the tail so the lobster is split in two lengthwise. Discard the stomach sacs and the greenish livers. Crack the lobster claw with the back of the knife. Rinse both halves under cold running water. Blot dry with paper towel.

2 Preheat the barbecue grill to medium direct heat.

3 Cook the lobsters, shell-side-down, for 10–12 minutes until the flesh becomes opaque.

4 Meanwhile, heat the butter over a low heat in a small saucepan. When melted, add the chili, garlic, orange peel and juice, and thyme leaves. Let the mixture sizzle for a few seconds, then remove from the heat. Season to taste and keep warm.

Serves 2

5 Serve the lobsters drizzled with a little of the butter mixture and sprinkled with the parsley. Serve any extra butter sauce separately.

game
on the grill

GAME FOR ANYTHING

It's safe to say that one of the earliest forms of barbecue cooking would have resulted from a wild game hunting expedition. Our ancestors discovered the magical benefits of cooking food over an open fire thousands of years ago; however, since these far-off times, this core task of survival has evolved over the centuries into a supremely pleasurable lifestyle activity.

For many people, there is nothing quite like the thrill of being out in the open air, and spending the day hunting for rabbit, deer, wild duck, pheasant, quail and other wild game. Moreover, the prospect of cooking wild food outdoors on the barbecue promises an extra bonus—especially when trying out the selection of tempting recipes featured here.

More of us live in cities nowadays, and you certainly don't have to be a fully fledged hunting, fishing and shooting type to savor this delicious fare. In fact, wild food such as game is becoming increasingly highly valued by city types for its purity, lack of additives, and for its lean, low-fat benefits. So, if you want to enjoy the benefits of eating game, you can find it at various specialist butchers and major supermarkets.

Much of our game is now intensively 'farmed', making it readily available all year round. Though purists feel that farmed game does not really match the unique flavor of food caught in the wild, it does have a distinctive taste; and this is why many people seek it out. In contrast to meat and poultry, game is very strongly-flavored. This is especially true of game birds such as pheasants that have been 'hung'. This means that they have been left to hand in a cool, dry place for a few days. This process actually helps to improve the meat—it releases natural enzymes into the flesh, and these cause a chemical change that 'tenderizes' the meat and imparts that characteristic 'gamey' flavor. The longer the meat has been 'hung', the stronger its flavor.

While the leanness of game meat constitutes a major health benefit, this

characteristic can also make it a little tricky to cook. The abundance of fat in other meats such as beef, pork and lamb acts as a natural moistening agent; with the exception of duck, game does not have this advantage, so the recipes here use clever devices such as sauces and marinades to keep the meat mouth-wateringly tender.

Apart from there being an immediate link between food caught in the wild and then cooked quickly out there in the open air, the hot and spicy barbecue recipes featured here are perfectly suited to the robust flavor of game—strongly flavored meats such as venison, rabbit and pheasant are not overwhelmed by strong seasonings. On the contrary—they taste even more exciting. You can't beat the great outdoors as a backdrop for the most memorable meal-times, so, whether you're tempted by Spicy Buffalo Burgers, Venison Steaks with Roasted Chili Butter or melt-in-your mouth Maple-Glazed Duck Breasts, these great recipes will revive your zest for living, and encourage you to get outdoors and cook up a feast!

Duck tortillas with sour orange and chili mop

Duck breasts are delicious, but don't try to cook them over direct heat—the fat will drip onto the coals and they will catch fire. Cooked over an indirect heat with a flavorful mop, they make a welcome change from the usual chicken or beef tortillas.

Serves 4

sour orange and chili mop
½ cup/ 125ml fresh orange juice
finely grated peel 1 orange
juice of ½ lemon
1 chipotle adobado, chopped plus
  1 tbsp of adobo sauce from the jar
2 large duck breasts

mango salsa
1 medium ripe mango
1 small red onion, finely chopped
1 small hot red chili, seeded and
  finely chopped
1 small tomato, seeded and
  finely chopped
1 lime, juice only
2 tbsp chopped fresh cilantro (coriander)
8 flour tortillas
salt and freshly ground black pepper

1 Preheat the barbecue to high indirect heat.

2 In a jug or small bowl, mix together the orange juice and peel, lemon juice and the chopped chipotle and adobo sauce. Set aside.

3 Peel the mango and remove the flesh in two large pieces by slicing either side of the flat stone that lies in the middle of the fruit. Chop the flesh finely and mix together in a small bowl with the onion, chili, tomato, lime juice and chopped cilantro (coriander). Season with salt and pepper and set aside.

4 To prepare the duck, lay skin side up on a cutting board. Using a small, sharp knife, make a series of slashes through the skin and into the fat but not into the meat. Make the slashes about ½ in/1 cm apart. Turn the meat a quarter turn and repeat the slashes so that you end up with a diamond pattern on the skin.

5 Cook the duck breasts, first skin side down, for 8-12 minutes, turning once and brushing often with the orange mop sauce. Cook for the shorter time for rare and the longer time for well done.

6 Meanwhile, wrap the tortillas in foil and place on the grill to warm through for 3-4 minutes.

7 To serve, remove the duck breasts from the heat and allow to cool slightly. Slice thickly and serve with the tortillas and mango salsa.

Maple-glazed duck breasts with chili pineapple relish

Duck has a great deal more flavor and a finer texture than many other fowl. It is best served slightly pink. Here it is teamed with a sweet glaze that is balanced by the heat and sharpness of the fruity relish.

2 large duck breasts or 4 duckling breasts
4 tbsp maple syrup
2 tbsp lemon juice

chili pineapple relish
1 small onion, finely chopped
1 small hot red chili, seeded and finely
  chopped
1 garlic clove, finely chopped
425g/15oz canned crushed pineapple or
  pineapple pieces
3/4 cup/125g lightly packed brown sugar
1¼ cups/300ml white wine vinegar
salt and freshly ground black pepper

1 Put all the ingredients for the pineapple relish except salt and pepper into a large saucepan. Heat gently until the sugar has completely dissolved, then bring to a boil and simmer rapidly until most of the vinegar has evaporated. If you drag a wooden spoon through the mixture, the bottom of the pan should stay visible and not fill with liquid. Remove from the heat and leave to cool.

2 To prepare the duck, lay skin side up on a cutting board. Using a small, sharp knife, make a series of slashes through the skin and

Serves 4

into the fat but not into the meat. Make the slashes about ½ in/1 cm apart. Turn the meat a quarter turn and repeat the slashes so that you end up with a diamond pattern on the skin. Set aside.

3 Preheat the barbecue to indirect medium heat.

4 Mix together the maple syrup, lemon juice and soy sauce. Set aside.

5 Cook the duck breasts, first skin side down, for 8-12 minutes, turning once and brushing during the last couple of minutes with the maple syrup mixture. Cook for the shorter time for duckling breasts and the longer time for larger duck breasts.

6 Remove from the heat and allow to rest for 5 minutes. Slice and serve with the chili pineapple relish.

Blackened grill-roasted venison

Despite the name of this dish, it's best to cook the meat until the spice mixture just darkens! And you must reduce the heat before the mixture burns, because it will become acrid if overcooked. Don't be tempted to cook the meat for too long—venison can easily dry out as it is so lean.

2 tsp salt
2 tsp paprika
1 tsp black, white and cayenne pepper
1 tsp dried thyme
1 tsp dried oregano
1lb/450g venison tenderloin
2 tbsp olive oil or vegetable oil

1 Preheat the barbecue grill to high direct heat.

2 In a small bowl, mix together the salt, paprika, peppers, thyme, and oregano.

3 Wash and dry the venison. Sprinkle the spice mixture onto a large plate or clean work surface. Roll the tenderloin in the spice mixture until well coated, pressing it down well to make sure the spices adhere evenly. Rub with the oil.

4 Cook the venison for 3–4 minutes, turning often, until the spice mixture darkens. Continue to cook over high direct heat for a total of 15–18 minutes, turning the meat regularly (15 minutes for medium-rare). Remove from the heat and let stand for 5 minutes before slicing. Serve immediately.

Venison steaks with roasted chili butter

As venison is a very lean meat, steaks are sometimes supplied 'larded', which means that the butcher injects fat into the meat to keep it moist during cooking.

1 long red chili
½ cup/120g unsalted butter, softened
2 tbsp chopped fresh cilantro (coriander)
4 venison steaks, 6–8oz/175-225g each
salt and freshly ground black pepper

1 Preheat the barbecue grill to medium direct heat.

2 Cook the chili over direct heat for about 5 minutes, turning often, until the skin has blackened. Put the chili into a small plastic bag and leave until cool enough to handle.

3 Peel the skin from the cooled chili. Remove the seeds and chop the flesh roughly.

4 Put the butter into a medium bowl and add the chopped chili and cilantro (coriander), and season to taste. Mix together thoroughly. Scrape the mixture onto a piece of plastic wrap (cling film) and shape into a log. Refrigerate until needed. (The butter can be prepared up to this point ahead of time and frozen or refrigerated until needed.)

5 Cook the venison steaks over medium direct heat for 6–8 minutes, turning once, until medium rare. Season to taste. Remove from the heat and let rest for 5 minutes. Remove the butter from the refrigerator and slice thickly. Put the steaks on individual serving dishes and top each one with 1 or 2 slices of the flavored butter. Serve immediately.

Serves 4

Stuffed pheasant with ranchero sauce

The stuffing and sauce in this recipe are also very good with chicken.

1 tsp cumin seeds
1 tsp coriander seeds
2 tbsp/25g butter
1 small onion, finely chopped
1 garlic clove
1 jalapeño chili, seeded and finely chopped
12oz/375g portabella, field or brown
  mushrooms, roughly chopped
3oz/75g cubed white bread
3 tbsp chopped fresh cilantro (coriander)
1 egg, lightly beaten
2 pheasants, about 1½-2lb/675g-900g each
6 slices bacon
salt and freshly ground black pepper

ranchero sauce

5 long green chilies
  (Anaheim or Mexican chilies)
2 tbsp olive oil
1 small onion, finely chopped
1 garlic clove, finely chopped
1 jalapeño chili, seeded and finely chopped
1½ lb/675g ripe tomatoes, peeled and
  chopped, or 2 cups
  (800g) canned plum
  tomatoes
½ tsp dried
  oregano

Serves 4

112

1 Preheat the barbecue grill to medium indirect heat.

2 To make the stuffing, put the cumin and coriander seeds into a small dry frying pan over a high heat. Heat until just smoking and the seeds starting to pop, shaking the pan occasionally. Remove the seeds from the pan and let cool slightly before grinding to a powder. Set aside.

3 Heat the butter over a medium heat in a large frying pan and when foaming, add the onion. Cook, stirring occasionally, for 5 minutes until softened. Add the garlic and chili and cook for a another 30 seconds before adding the mushrooms. Increase the heat and cook for about 5-7 minutes until the mushrooms have softened. Add the ground roasted spices and stir briefly. Transfer the mixture to a large mixing bowl and let cool for about 5 minutes.

4 Add the cubed bread, cilantro (coriander), and egg along with seasoning. Mix thoroughly and set aside.

5 Wash the pheasants inside and out and dry thoroughly with paper towels. Stuff the birds with the mushroom mixture. Season the skin of the birds and lay the bacon slices over the breasts.

6 Cook the pheasants over indirect medium heat for 50-60 minutes, until the juices run clear. The leg should also pull easily away from the body—if in doubt, cook for a further 10 minutes, then test again.

7 Meanwhile, make the ranchero sauce. Roast the long green chilies over direct heat alongside the pheasant for about 5 minutes, turning often, until the skin has blackened. Remove the chilies to a plastic bag until cool enough to handle. Peel off the blackened skin, remove the seeds and chop the flesh finely. Set aside.

8 Heat the oil over a medium heat in a large saucepan and add the onion, garlic, and jalapeño chili. Cook for about 5 minutes until softened. Add the tomatoes, oregano, and chopped roasted chilies. Bring to a boil and simmer, uncovered, for 45 minutes until thickened, stirring occasionally. If using canned tomatoes, 30 minutes may be long enough. Season to taste and keep warm.

9 To serve, remove the pheasant from the barbecue and allow to rest for 10 minutes. Remove the bacon slices (serve them separately) and carve the bird as you would a chicken. Leave the drumstick, however, as it has little meat and will be stringy. Serve immediately with the sauce.

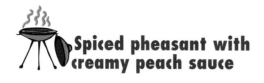

Spiced pheasant with creamy peach sauce

Hen pheasants tend to be more tender and are better for grilling—use the male pheasants to make excellent casseroles.

Serves 4

2 small hen pheasants, about 1½-2lb/675g-900g each
pinch of saffron strands
½ tsp cayenne pepper
½ tsp ground cumin
1 tsp ground coriander
½ tsp ground cinnamon
2 tbsp vegetable or olive oil
salt and freshly ground black pepper

creamy peach sauce
1 tbsp olive oil
1 small onion, finely chopped
1¾ cups (400g can) peach halves in juice, drained and roughly chopped
1 small jalapeño chili, seeded and finely chopped
¾ cup/185ml chicken stock
3 tbsp sour cream or crème fraîche
2 tbsp snipped fresh chives
2 tbsp chopped fresh cilantro (coriander)

1 Preheat the barbecue grill to medium direct heat.

2 Joint each pheasant into 4 pieces as follows: Using a sharp knife or heavy quality kitchen scissors, cut down either side of the backbone and remove. Cut the bird in half through the breastbone. Remove the leg quarters. You should have 8 pieces.

3 Crush the saffron strands to a powder using a pestle and mortar. Add the cayenne pepper, cumin, coriander, and cinnamon and mix together. Season to taste.

4 Put the pheasant pieces on a plate and sprinkle with the spice mixture. Rub the mixture into the skin. Let marinate for 30 minutes.

5 Brush the meat with the olive or vegetable oil. Cook over direct medium heat. The legs will need about 10–12 minutes and the breasts about 12–15 minutes. Turn the pieces once or twice during cooking until golden and the juices run clear. Remove from the heat and let rest for 10 minutes.

6 Meanwhile, make the creamy peach sauce. Heat a medium-size frying pan over medium heat. Add the olive oil and when hot, add the onion. Cook for 7-8 minutes until softened and lightly browned. Add the peach pieces and jalapeño chili and cook for a further 2-3 minutes.

7 Add the chicken stock and bring to a boil. Simmer rapidly for 10 minutes until slightly reduced. Lower the heat and stir in the sour cream. Bring to a boil again, then simmer gently for 2 minutes.

8 Stir in the chives and cilantro (coriander) and season to taste. Serve immediately with the pheasant.

Butterflied quail rubbed with ginger, cumin, and coriander

If you get some quail, try this recipe. They are tasty little birds, and are easy to prepare and quick to cook. They're a perfect size to eat with your fingers, so it's best to provide finger bowls and plenty of napkins.

8 quail
1 tsp ground ginger
1 tsp ground cumin
2 tsp ground coriander
2 tsp chopped dried guajillo chili
2 tsp salt
1 tsp coarsely ground black pepper
2 tbsp vegetable or olive oil
green (spring) onions, finely sliced, to garnish
lemon wedges, to serve

1 Preheat the barbecue grill to medium direct heat.

2 In a small bowl, mix together the ginger, cumin, coriander, chili, salt, and pepper. Set aside.

3 Using kitchen scissors, cut the birds open down the backbone and lay them, skin-side-up, on a cutting board. Press down on the breastbone to flatten the bird. Sprinkle over the spice mixture and rub thoroughly into the birds on all sides. Set aside to marinate for 30 minutes.

4 To butterfly the birds, push a metal or wooden skewer through the drumstick on one side and out through the wing on the other side. Repeat to have 2 crossed skewers through the bird holding it flat.

5 Brush the quail with the vegetable or olive oil and cook, skin-side-down first, for 15–20 minutes, turning 2 or 3 times, until golden and the juices run clear. Serve garnished with the sliced green (spring) onions and lemon wedges.

Serves 4

115

Crispy-skinned oriental spiced quail

These birds require a little preparation before barbecuing to give lots of flavor and a crispy skin.

8 quail
3 tbsp Sichuan peppercorns
2 tbsp salt
2 green (spring) onions, finely chopped
3 slices fresh ginger
1 tbsp rice wine
3 tbsp soy sauce
2 tbsp granulated sugar

1 Preheat the barbecue grill to high direct heat.

2 Prepare the quail as in step 4 of Butterflied Quail (see page 115) but do not skewer the birds. Instead, cut them in half through the breastbone to give 16 pieces. Dry with paper towels, if necessary—they should be as dry as possible.

3 Fry the Sichuan peppercorns over low heat in a small dry frying pan for about 2 minutes until brown and aromatic. Add the salt and fry 1 more minute. Place in a bowl and let cool.

4 Grind the peppercorn mixture until fairly fine. Reserving about 1½ tbsp for serving, rub the quail pieces all over with the peppercorn mixture. Let stand for 6 hours or overnight, if possible.

6 Meanwhile, mix together the green (spring) onions, ginger, rice wine, and soy sauce. Let macerate while marinating the quails.

6 Strain the soy sauce mixture and discard the ginger and green (spring) onions. Brush the quail pieces thoroughly with the strained soy sauce mixture. Cook first, skin-side-down, for 8–10 minutes turning twice until the skin is browned and crisp and the juices run clear.

6 Serve immediately with the reserved peppercorn mixture.

Serves 4

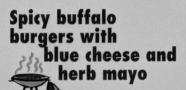

Spicy buffalo burgers with blue cheese and herb mayo

Buffalo meat has more flavor than beef and is lower in fat, so why not try it? If you can't find buffalo, though, ground beef is a good substitute.

1½lb/675g ground buffalo

2 tbsp caribe (guajillo chili flakes) or ancho chili powder

2 tsp ground cumin

2 tsp garlic salt

1 tsp brown sugar

1 tsp freshly ground black pepper

1 onion, thickly sliced

2 tsp olive oil

¼ cup/55g blue cheese, crumbled

1 tbsp chopped fresh mixed herbs, such as chives, basil, and parsley

½ quantity Homemade Mayonnaise (see page 141) or ¾ cup/175ml ready-made mayonnaise

4 burger buns, split, to serve

1 Preheat the barbecue grill to medium direct heat.

2 Put the buffalo meat into a large bowl and add the chili powder, cumin, garlic salt, sugar, and black pepper. Mix together well (your hands are best for this) and shape into 4 equal portions. Flatten the patties to about ¾ inch/2cm thick. Set aside.

3 Brush the onion slices with the olive oil. Lay them on the grill over direct heat. Cook for 2—3 minutes, turn, then add the burgers. Cook the onions for 8–10 minutes, turning often until golden and tender, and cook the burgers for about 8 minutes total, turning once, for medium-rare. Add another 1-2 minutes if you prefer them well done.

4 Meanwhile, mix the cheese and fresh herbs into the mayonnaise and set aside.

5 Toast the buns and transfer to a serving plate. Top each bun with a burger, an onion slice and a dollop of the mayonnaise.

Olive, chili and herb-stuffed rabbit legs

Unless you know how to do it yourself, it's probably best to get your butcher to bone the rabbit legs for you.

Serves 4

4 large rabbit legs, or 8 small legs, bone removed
½ cup/50g pitted, mixed black and green olives, finely chopped
2 garlic cloves, crushed
3 tbsp chopped fresh parsley
3 tbsp chopped fresh cilantro (coriander)
1 tbsp chopped chipotles in adobo
peel of ½ lemon
4 or 8 slices smoked bacon (depending on how many legs you are using)
salt and freshly ground black pepper

1 Preheat the barbecue grill to medium indirect heat.

2 Season the rabbit legs with salt and pepper. Set aside.

3 In a medium mixing bowl, mix together the olives, garlic, parsley, cilantro (coriander), chipotles in adobo, and lemon peel. Season to taste.

4 Divide the olive mixture between the rabbit legs, filling the gap where the bone used to be. Wrap the meat round the stuffing. Using the back edge of a knife, stretch the bacon rashers by pressing along their length. Wrap a slice of bacon round the stuffed portion of each leg and secure with toothpicks (cocktail sticks), if necessary.

5 Cook over medium indirect heat for 15–20 minutes, turning 2–3 times until golden and the juices run clear. Be careful not to overcook or the legs will become dry. Serve immediately.

Spicy marinated rabbit with cider and prunes

Being a lean meat, rabbit benefits from being cooked in a sauce, and marinating it first also adds tenderness. Here, the combination of sweet and spicy makes a really tasty barbecue stew. Get your butcher to joint the rabbit for you into even-size pieces.

8oz/225g baby onions, peeled
2 carrots, roughly chopped
2 celery stalks, roughly chopped
3 cups/750ml hard cider
1 bay leaf, crumbled
3 pasillo chilies (or other hot, dried variety),
  lightly pounded
1 large rabbit, about 4lb/2kg,
  jointed into 8 pieces
1 cup/125g pitted prunes, roughly chopped
3 tbsp crème fraîche
2 tbsp chopped fresh parsley
salt and freshly ground black pepper

1 Preheat the barbecue to medium indirect heat.

2 Bring a medium saucepan of water to a boil and plunge in the baby onions. Bring the water back to a boil and immediately drain. Refresh under cold running water and drain again.

3 Put the onions, carrots, celery, cider, bay leaf, and chilies into a large bowl. Add the rabbit pieces and turn well. Cover and marinate overnight.

4 Remove the rabbit from the marinade. Cook the rabbit pieces for 5 minutes over the direct heat part of the barbecue until golden on all sides. Meanwhile, put the marinade and vegetables into a large saucepan and bring to a boil (this will speed up the process—if you leave out this step, add another 20–30 minutes cooking time on the barbecue).

5 Put a large aluminum foil tray or roasting pan onto the barbecue grill ensuring it isn't directly over the heat. Transfer the rabbit pieces to the tray and carefully pour the hot marinade over. Add the prunes. Cover loosely with aluminum foil or top with a second aluminum foil tray which is turned upside down. Cook over medium indirect heat for 1½–2 hours until the rabbit is very tender.

6 Carefully remove the aluminum foil container or roasting pan. Strain the sauce into a saucepan. Put the rabbit and vegetables into a large serving bowl and keep warm. Bring the sauce to a boil and simmer until reduced to ½ cup/125ml. Add the crème fraîche and simmer for another minute. Season to taste. Pour the sauce over the rabbit and vegetables, and sprinkle with the parsley. Serve immediately.

veg n' Side Orders

GRILL UP THE VEGETABLES

It's easy to forget that you can cook lots of different foods on your barbecue in addition to the usual meat and fish dishes. Vegetables are an excellent example—they are utterly delicious when grilled—and once you've enjoyed the delights of eating your own, char-broiled favorites, you'll soon realize what you've been missing.

Grilled vegetables are now highly fashionable, reflecting the mellow influences of Mediterranean cooking all around the world. There's something so simple and so satisfying in seeing a dazzling display of vegetables such as bright yellow corn cobs, yellow, red and green bell peppers, deep purple eggplants, scarlet tomatoes and golden squash sizzling away on the grill. You can broil a whole gardenful of goodies, including zucchini, asparagus, artichokes, mushrooms, onions and potatoes. Apart from being scrumptious in their own right, they make fine accompaniments to your grilled meats.

PREPARING TO GRILL

Remember, this is light, informal cooking—you don't have to make too much fuss about presentation. After cleaning and preparing your vegetables as usual (by cutting away any hard stems, roots, or tough outer leaves, and cutting or slicing into grill-size pieces) they are pretty much ready to go straight onto the grill. However, it's a good idea to give them a coating of light olive oil to protect them from drying. As for seasoning, why not try one of these suggestions? Simply add a sprinkling of rosemary, parsley, basil, thyme, garlic, freshly ground black pepper, or salt—the choice is yours.

NATURAL FLAVORING AGENTS

Many vegetables contain powerfully aromatic volatile oils—chilies, peppers and onions are obvious examples. You can take clever advantage of this when you're cooking meat on the grill. You know that certain woods such as hickory, mesquite or oak impart different flavors to the broiling meat or fish; but

124

the same applies to vegetables, too. So, if you haven't got any specialized smoking woods at hand, one of the best ways of wafting flavor around the meat is by cooking vegetables beneath it.

Take onions, for instance—they're convenient and easily available. Chop a couple of medium-size onions into large pieces, coat them lightly in olive oil, then wrap them in heavy duty aluminum foil. Now, position the parcel somewhere on the fire so that the onions begin to cook very slowly. In just a few minutes, enticing aromas will be filling the air. They willl also be penetrating the meat

cooking on the grill, of course, and will give it the most delicious flavor. Your parcel also provides a mouth-watering mini feast! Take it from the coals before the onions are overcooked, and enjoy snacking on the contents while you finish your barbecue. As you get more experienced, you'll discover the best place to position your vegetable parcels. Try using garlic, bell peppers, large chilies experiment in mix-and-match combinations.

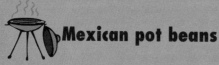

Mexican pot beans

These classic Southwestern-style beans are so versatile—keep a pot in the fridge to make refried beans or purée and serve as a dip with fresh tortilla chips. They're also good with plain grilled meat and fish.

2 cups/500g dried pinto beans
1 onion, finely chopped
3oz/75g smoked bacon, chopped
2 dried red chilies, roughly chopped
2 garlic cloves, roughly chopped
1 bay leaf, crumbled
1 tbsp salt
freshly ground black pepper

1 Put the pinto beans into a large bowl and pick them over, removing any little stones or beans that are shriveled or discolored. Cover the beans with at least twice their volume of cold water and leave to soak overnight.

2 Next day, drain the beans and put into a large saucepan (one that is tall and deep is best as it will reduce evaporation of water). Add the onion, bacon, chilies, garlic, and bay leaf and cover with water by about 3–4 in/7.5–10cms (about 6–8 cups/1.5–2lt).

3 Bring slowly to a boil, skimming off any residue that rises to the surface. When boiling, reduce the heat, cover, and simmer very gently for 2 hours.

4 Add 1 tbsp salt and continue to cook the beans, uncovered, for another 1 hour or until they are very tender and the liquid is very thick. Taste for seasoning and add more salt, if necessary, and black pepper. Serve immediately or cool and refrigerate for up to 3 days.

Serves 4–6

REFRIED BEANS

In a large, nonstick frying pan, heat about 2 tbsp of olive oil. Add 2 cups/500ml of Pot Beans and crush them using a potato masher or fork. Repeat twice more, adding 1 cup/250ml Pot Beans at a time until the purée is thick and creamy. Serve immediately.

 # Cornbread

Cornbread is the ideal accompaniment to grilled foods. It is best eaten while still warm, so shouldn't be made too far in advance.

1 cup/120g all-purpose flour
1¼ cups/150g fine cornmeal
3 tbsp granulated sugar
2½ tsp baking powder
½ tsp salt
2 tbsp chopped fresh thyme
2 eggs
1 cup/250ml buttermilk

2 tbsp melted butter
salt and freshly ground pepper

1 Preheat the oven to 400°F/200°C, Gas 6. Mix together the flour, cornmeal, sugar, baking powder, salt, and most of the thyme, reserving about one third for decoration. In a separate bowl, beat the eggs, then stir in the buttermilk and butter.

2 Pour the wet ingredients onto the flour mixture and stir just enough to combine. Spoon into a buttered and lined 8 inch/20cm square cake tin. Sprinkle over remaining thyme. Transfer to the oven and bake for 30 minutes until golden and risen or until a toothpick inserted into the center comes out clean. Cut into squares to serve.

Serves 6

Variation
PUMPKIN SEED AND GREEN CHILI CORNBREAD
To the dry ingredients, add generous 1/2 cup/75g toasted pumpkin seeds which have been roughly chopped. To the wet ingredients, add 2 finely chopped green chilies and replace the buttermilk with sour cream. Omit the thyme. Bake as above.

CRANBERRY CORNBREAD
Fold 1 1/2 cups/125g fresh cranberries into the batter before baking as above, omitting the thyme leaves.

Spiced grilled sweet potatoes

Too often sweet potatoes are served with extra sugar. Try this savory version and you'll never go back to marshmallow-topped concoctions again.

Serves 4

4 medium sweet potatoes
(about 1½ lb/675g)
2 tbsp olive oil
1 tsp crushed chilies
½ tsp ground cinnamon
2 garlic cloves, crushed
salt and freshly
ground black pepper

1 Preheat the barbecue grill to medium direct heat.

2 Cut the sweet potatoes, without peeling them, lengthwise into 8 wedges each. Put the remaining ingredients into a large bowl and mix together. Season to taste. Add the potato wedges and mix gently until coated in the spices and oil.

3 Grill the potato wedges, cut-side-down over direct heat for 8–10 minutes, turning once, until tender and golden. Watch the potatoes carefully— they can burn very easily because of their high sugar content. Serve immediately.

Grilled corn cobs with flavored butter

Mmm! Oozing with butter and scented with fragrant herbs, these transform a traditional accompaniment into some thing really special.

½ cup/ 120g unsalted butter, softened
1 hot green chili, seeded and finely chopped
½ tsp ground cumin
1 tsp ground coriander
2 tbsp chopped fresh cilantro (coriander)
8 corn cobs, husks intact
salt and freshly ground black pepper

1 Preheat the barbecue grill to medium direct heat.

2 Put the butter into a medium bowl and beat with a fork or wooden spoon until smooth. Add the chili, cumin, coriander, cilantro (coriander), and seasoning. Mix together thoroughly. Set aside.

3 Carefully peel back the husks of the corn, without removing them. Pull off the silk threads, removing as much as possible. Spread each cob with about 2 tbsp of the butter mixture, then carefully fold the husk back up over each cob. Tie securely with string at the top.

4 Grill the corn over direct medium heat for 8–10 minutes, turning occasionally, until the corn is lightly and evenly browned. Serve immediately.

Serves 4

VARIATIONS
Spread with Garlic and Herb Butter (see page 96); Orange Chili Butter (see page 102); Chipotle, Lime & Coriander Mayo (see page 88); or Roasted Chili Butter (see page 111).

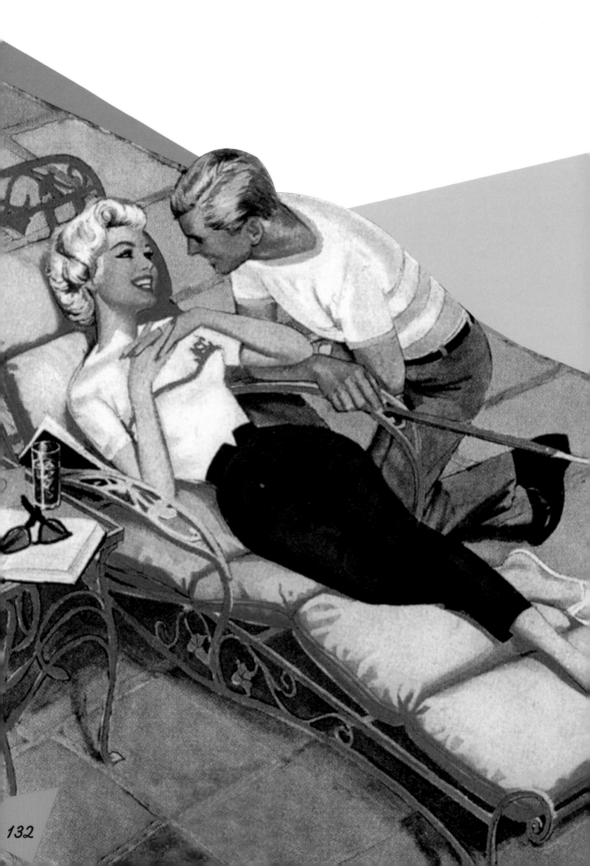

Spicy grilled potato wedges

These are the quickest, tastiest and lowest-fat chips you'll find—and they're good with just about anything.

1 tbsp olive oil
1 tbsp chili seasoning mix
2 garlic cloves, crushed
  2¼lb/ 1kg potatoes, skins left on
    salt and freshly ground black
      pepper

1 Preheat the barbecue grill to medium direct heat.

2 In a large bowl, mix together the olive oil, chili seasoning, and garlic. Cut the potatoes into large chunks or wedges and add them to the bowl. Stir to coat the potatoes in the oil mixture.

3 Lay the potato wedges on the barbecue grill over direct heat and cook for 12–15 minutes, turning once, until tender and golden. Serve immediately.

Mixed vegetable grill

These vegetables are delicious hot as an accompaniment to grilled meats and fish, or served at room temperature as a salad with fresh goat's cheese and crusty bread.

6 portabella mushrooms, wiped

2 medium zucchini (courgettes), each cut
   lengthwise into 3 slices

2 red onions, peeled and each cut
   lengthwise into 6 wedges

9oz/250g fresh asparagus, trimmed

1 medium eggplant (aubergine), cut
   crosswise into ½ inch/1cm thick slices

3 plum tomatoes, halved lengthwise

6 tbsp olive oil

2 tbsp balsamic vinegar

3 tbsp chopped fresh basil

salt and freshly ground black
   pepper

1 Preheat the barbecue grill to high direct heat.

2 Brush all the vegetables with a little of the olive oil. Cook over high direct heat for 5–8 minutes or until tender and golden (the tomatoes may take less time, while the onion and the mushrooms may take longer).

3 Meanwhile, in a small pan, heat the remaining olive oil with the balsamic vinegar, basil, and seasoning to taste until just sizzling. Remove immediately from the heat and set aside.

Serves 6

4 Transfer the vegetables as they cook to a large serving platter. When they are all cooked, pour the oil and balsamic vinegar mixture over the top. Serve immediately or let cool and serve at room temperature.

Texas pilaf

This very fragrant, lightly spiced rice dish is the perfect accompaniment to any grilled meat or fish. You can simply adjust the amount of chili according to personal taste.

1½ cups/320g basmati or Texmati rice
1 tbsp olive oil
1 onion, finely chopped
1 green chili, seeded and finely chopped
1 garlic clove, finely chopped
2 tsp cumin seeds
1 large tomato, peeled and roughly chopped

2 cups/500ml chicken stock
2 tbsp chopped fresh cilantro (coriander)
salt and freshly ground black pepper

1 Put the rice into a large bowl and wash it in several changes of cold water until the water runs relatively clear. Put the rice into a strainer and let drain while you prepare the remaining ingredients.

Serves 4

2 Heat the oil over a medium heat in a large saucepan or flameproof casserole with a tight-fitting lid. When hot, add the onion, chili, and garlic. Cook, stirring occasionally, for 5–7 minutes until the onion begins to brown. Add the cumin seeds and stir for another 30 seconds or so.

3 Add the tomato and cook for another 1 minute until softened. Add the drained rice and stir well to coat in the oil and tomato.

4 Add the stock and bring to a boil. Reduce the heat as low as possible and cover tightly. Simmer over the lowest heat for 15 minutes, then remove from the heat and let stand without lifting the lid for a further 10 minutes.

5 Just before serving, add the cilantro (coriander) and season to taste. Serve immediately.

Coleslaw with jalapeño and mango

Serves 6

This salad makes an unusual and refreshing change to coleslaw. The sweetness of the mango helps to balance the fiery jalapeño. If you prefer, you can use pineapple instead.

1 cup/225g Homemade Mayonnaise
  (page 141), or ready-made
2 jalapeño chilies, seeded and finely
  chopped
4 green (spring) onions, finely chopped
1 large carrot, finely grated
1 tbsp lemon juice
2 tsp Dijon mustard
1 tsp sugar
1 green cabbage, about 1¼ lb/500g
1 small ripe mango
salt and freshly ground black pepper

1 Put the mayonnaise into a large bowl. Add the chilies, green (spring) onions, carrot, lemon juice, Dijon mustard, and sugar and mix together thoroughly. Season to taste.

2 Halve the cabbage through the core, then quarter. Remove the core, then slice the cabbage thinly. Add to the bowl with the dressing.

3 Peel the mango and remove the flesh in 2 large pieces by slicing either side of the flat stone that lies in the middle of the fruit. Chop finely and add to the cabbage in the bowl.

4 Mix together gently but thoroughly and taste for seasoning.

NOTE
This salad can be served immediately but the flavor improves if left for an hour or longer. Refrigerate if not using straight away.

NOTE

This recipe contains raw eggs and should be used on the day it is made or kept refrigerated for no more than one day.

Homemade mayonnaise

This recipe uses a mixture of olive oil and vegetable oil, which gives the mayonnaise a more delicate flavor than when it is made using extra virgin olive oil alone. The amount of lemon juice or vinegar needed will depend on personal taste, but aim for a mayonnaise that is smooth with a slight sharpness and that doesn't taste oily—if it does, add a little more lemon or vinegar.

Makes 1½ cups/ 375ml

1 large egg yolk
2 tsp Dijon mustard
about 1 tbsp lemon juice or white wine
  vinegar
¾ cup/185ml olive oil
½ cup/125ml vegetable oil
salt and freshly ground black pepper

1 In a food processor, or in the jug of a stick blender, whisk together the egg yolk, mustard, lemon juice or vinegar, and seasoning until foamy.

2 With the motor running, gradually add the olive and vegetable oils in a very slow but steady stream until all the oil is added and the mixture is thick and pale. Taste and add more lemon juice or vinegar as necessary. If the mixture is too thick, add about 1 tbsp hot water until thinned to the desired consistency.

Index

Picture Credits